THE SACRED WRITINGS

The sixty adventures of Sherlock Holmes, as re-corded by John H. Watson, M.D., are classics in their genre and, as such, have spawned hundreds of volumes of expert analysis and literary study. None, however, has withstood the test of time as well as this warm and imaginative re-creation of the legendary master detective.

Though not intended to be a scholarly treatise, this work contains a great deal of valuable information about both Conan Doyle and the Holmes stories— "The Sacred Writings," as the Baker Street Ir-regulars refer to them. Here, too, is fascination and entertainment that will endure as long as the cold London fog rolls in with the winter and mischief is planned and thwarted, and books are written and read.

Come, visit once again "the nostalgic country of the mind, where it is always 1895."

THE
PRIVATE
LIFE
OF

SHERLOCK
HOLMES

BY
VINCENT
STARRETT

PINNACLE BOOKS • NEW YORK CITY

IN MEMORIAM

Arthur Conan Doyle

William Gillette

Frederic Dorr Steele

Gray Chandler Briggs

H. W. Bell

Alexander Woollcott

Elmer Davis

Christopher Morley

Basil Rathbone

ACKNOWLEDGMENTS

It would be difficult, not to say impossible, to acknowledge every published line which may have influenced the author's thought in the making of this book; but one's gratitude is chiefly due a certain John H. Watson, M.D., sometime of 221B Baker Street, London, England. More precisely, one is grateful to his amanuensis, the late Sir Arthur Conan Doyle, and the estate of Sir Arthur, with whose gracious permission this volume was made possible. Formal—and grateful—acknowledgment is made also as follows: to Messrs. Harper & Brothers, publishers of *The Adventures of Sherlock Holmes* (Copyright 1892) and *The Memoirs of Sherlock Holmes* (Copyright 1894); to Messrs. Doubleday and Company, publishers of *The Hound of the Baskervilles* (Copyright 1902), *The Return of Sherlock Holmes* (Copyright 1905), *The Valley of Fear* (Copyright 1914), *His Last Bow* (Copyright 1917), and *The Case Book of Sherlock Holmes* (Copyright 1927); to Messrs. Little, Brown & Company, publishers of *Memories and Adventures*, by Arthur Conan Doyle; and again to Messrs. Doubleday and Company, publishers of *The Case of Oscar Slater*, by Arthur Conan Doyle.

Several of the present chapters appeared first in American journals, to the editors of which acknowledgment is made as follows: to the *Atlantic Monthly* for "Enter Mr. Sherlock Holmes"; to *Real Detective Tales* for "No. 221B Baker Street"; to the *Golden Book* for "The Real Sherlock Holmes"; and to the *Bookman* for "The Private Life of Sherlock Holmes" and "*Ave Sherlock Morituri et Cetera.*"

"The Singular Adventures of Martha Hudson" appeared first in *Baker Street Studies*, edited by H. W. Bell (London: Constable & Co., Ltd., 1934); subsequently in *Profile by Gaslight*, edited by Edgar W. Smith (New York: Simon & Schuster, 1944) and *Bookman's Holiday* by Vincent Starrett (New York: Random House, 1942).

"The Adventure of the Unique Hamlet" was first published by Walter M. Hill of Chicago in an edition of 200 copies (Christmas, 1920); it was reprinted in *221B: Studies in Sherlock Holmes*, edited by Vincent Starrett (New York: Macmillan Co., 1940), and *The Misadventures of Sherlock Holmes*, edited by Ellery Queen (Boston: Little, Brown & Co., 1944).

All but two of the present chapters were published in *The Private Life of Sherlock Holmes* (New York: Macmillan Co., 1933); these have been substantially rewritten for the present edition.

CONTENTS

INTRODUCTION

This is the most famous book about Sherlock Holmes
ever written. Perhaps I should say the most famous
biography. It may be that I should also exclude the
writings of Dr. Watson, without which, of course, there
would have been no Sherlock Holmes. But I think that
most Sherlockians would agree with me that this work
has been enormously influential and remains to this day
one of the most felicitous renderings on the subject of
the world's most celebrated private detective. And I, for
one, shall stick to my guns and say that this *is* the most
famous book about Holmes ever written. For, as Watson
was Holmes's amanuensis, Starrett was his Boswell: he
was also Mrs. Hudson's Boswell, and Watson's too, for
that matter. If you read Watson, you must perforce read
Starrett, thereby ordaining yourself an inveterate Sherlockian, or Holmesian, and most certainly a confirmed
Vincentian (one devoted to the work of Vincent Starrett,
the coinage "Starrettian" having no currency). Whatever order you choose in the reading, you will find yourself in remarkably sanguineous company, and, it follows,
respectably addicted. You will have gained an incor-
ruptible fondness for the medicine that is Sherlock

Holmes. And for that they cannot arrest you, no matter how much you ingest or disseminate.

Sherlock Holmes is the most popular fictional character in all of literature. Dr. Watson ranks second. In the ranking of writers on the two figures there has been much division and revision, but as *the* biographer I would advance Vincent Starrett as the principal claimant: not that he would so assert himself, or that he was the first to address himself to the subjects, but his *The Private Life of Sherlock Holmes* has been called the standard biography as well as the cornerstone of what is known as the "higher criticism." Some time ago H. Douglas Thompson said that "in the department of biography, I would give pride of place to Vincent Starrett." I will go even further than that. I also suspect that Sir Arthur himself would be among those who would readily advance the argument that Vincent Starrett is meritorious of "Conanization."

Starrett undertook his charming monographs on Holmes much earlier than is generally known. His notations indicate projections on them even prior to his first published essay on Holmes in 1918. Indeed, he had visualized a book on Holmes, a bibliography of Doyle, and even a "pastiche" that was *not* "The Unique Hamlet" (one of the most celebrated "pastiches"; Chapter 12 in this book). The point is made that Starrett approached Holmes with great originality of invention. He grew up with Holmes, after all (having been born in the same year the first Holmes story was written), and the effect was salubrious. The subject had been touched upon by such literary luminaries as Twain, Milne, Barrie, Robert Barr, and O'Henry. But they did not see Holmes in quite the way Starrett saw him, nor did they know him as well. They were, in effect, hawks and popinjays, whereas Starrett was always the bloody owl. In the beginning he was a solemn scholar on the subject, addressing Holmes in a refreshingly divergent way, and with a perspicacity and enthusiasm that no one else had approached. It was soon after his early published monograph in 1918 that they began to touch on what he was producing. I have dipped into a quantity of fine "post-Vincentian" commentaries on Holmes, only to discover that Starrett's work nourished both the borrowers and the lenders, the derivers and the innovators, and that some of both have been generous in acknowledging their indebtedness, while others conveniently sidestepped the courtesy of giving their source a name. The name was Starrett. It is still Starrett. And this work is still the masterpiece it has always been.

The present edition is the one to have. The first edition collector will want to own this, along with the 1933 Macmillan edition and the revised and enlarged edition of 1960 (University of Chicago). The present edition contains matter that does not appear in any of the editions preceding it, and one can hardly quarrel with the price that is placed on it.

In this book you will find the searching scholarship and charming style of Starrett. In this work he changed the entire posture of Sherlockian inquiry, fostering the grand illusion, as no one before him had done with comparable gusto, that Sherlock Holmes was a real person, and an imperishable one at that. The illusion was not merely a curious anomaly for Starrett. You will find his note on Balzac's "Let's get back to reality," when the French author intended his fictional character, Grandet. Holmes, for Starrett, was real in much the same way. Anyone who knew Starrett as the "Dean of Sherlockians" and the astute literary physician who brought so many neglected writers back to life, Crane and Machen and Bierce among them, understood the kind of realities that soared about the fertile terrain of his mountainous brain and gave him the experience of both heaven and hell that only men of rare genius know.

Starrett, the genius, captured those elusive realities on

the point of his pen, transferring them to paper with an indelible charm and vitality. And Starrett the man and writer revered Sherlock Holmes. He wrote about him as an admirable friend, with a respectful honesty, and in the writing he gave every structured sentence and paragraph the singular stamp of his marvelous style. This book is not only a stunning display of scholarship, it is a work that is eminently readable, of true originality and virtuosity, that glitters with wit and flashes of merriment, that stands solidly on a platform of wide-ranging discovery, that reverberates with the ring of verities that Starrett's perceptive mind appertained.

I shall not presume to prolong the anticipation of the reader who has not yet become acquainted with this classic, so that I defer to the man of genius who awaits your companionship.

Prosaic scholar that I am, I am honored to have been chosen to introduce this masterpiece, as I was honored and privileged to have been counted among the fortunate friends of the man who wrote it.

Michael Murphy
April, 1975

ENTER

MR.

SHERLOCK

HOLMES

The London "season" of the year 1886, on its surface, was much as other and similar seasons had been. No blare of sudden trumpets marked its advent. Victoria was still placidly upon her throne; Lord Salisbury—for the second time—had ousted Gladstone from the premier's chair; Ireland was seething with outrage and sedition; crime and poverty were widespread; and Beecham's Pills were "universally admitted to be a marvellous antidote for nervous disorders." In literature the gods, perhaps, were Stevenson and Meredith and Henty, depending upon one's age; but an Irishman named Wilde was making himself a freakish reputation by his championship of aestheticism. At the Gaiety, Mr. Cellier's *Dorothy* had begun its celebrated run of 968 performances, and *The Harbor Lights* were gleaming brightly at the Adelphi. In Piccadilly the race of hansom cabs was swift and dangerous. No wars immediately threatened; for the moment the wide world was at peace. And no celestial phenomena was noted to suggest that, once more in the history of the world, a blue moon was marking an epochal event. Certainly no planets fell to tell an impecunious provinicial doctor, resident at Southsea, Portsmouth, that he had brought forth a new immortal in the world of letters.

Sherlock Holmes, however, was already in the world. With a Dr. Watson, late of the 5th Northumberland Fusiliers, he had engaged a suite of rooms at No. 221B Baker Street, London, and entered upon his astonishing career as a consulting specialist in crime. As far as the world is concerned, he is there yet.

Times had not been of the best for Dr. A. Conan Doyle of Bush Villa, Southsea. The young man had recently married and was eking out the slender returns of early medical practice by writing stories for the magazines. It had occurred to him that he might go on writing short stories forever and make no headway. What was necessary, he was certain, if one intended to be an author, was to get one's name upon the cover of a book. A first novel—*The Firm of Girdlestone*—had failed to find a publisher and was still in manuscript about the house. But he had, for some time, been turning in his mind the possibility of something new and fresh in the literature of detection. Gaboriau had pleased him by the precision of his plots, and a boyhood hero had been the Chevalier C. Auguste Dupin, Poe's masterful amateur detective. What was there, he asked himself, that he—Doyle—could bring to this field which would be indubitably his own?

At night, outside over his door, burned the red lamp that was the sign of his profession. In the daylight, his brass nameplate—polished every morning—shone brightly in the Portsmouth sun. But the patients that either of them should have attracted were few and far between. In his patients' sitting room (three chairs, a table, and a patch of carpet), as he smoked and meditated, there rose before him the remembered image of his former teacher at the university, one Joseph Bell, "thin, wiry, dark, with a high-nosed acute face, penetrating grey eyes, angular shoulders," and a peculiar walk: Joseph Bell, M.D., F.R.C.S., Edinburgh; consulting surgeon to the Royal Infirmary and Royal Hospital for Sick Children, whose voice was high and discordant, whose skill as a surgeon was profound, and whose uncanny trick of diagnosis was a legend of the institution. It occurred to the young physician, waiting for the patients who did not come, that if Joseph Bell had determined to be a detective, he would have reduced "this fascinating but unorganized business to something nearer an exact science."

Bell, for reasons which Doyle the student had never quite understood, had singled him out from among the droves of others who frequented the wards, and made him his outpatient clerk. It was not an onerous position. The student herded the waiting patients into line, made simple notes of their cases, and ushered them into the big room in which Bell sat in state. But it had become quickly evident to young Arthur Conan Doyle that Joseph Bell learned more about the patients at a glance than he, the questioner, had learned with all his queries.

"He would sit in his receiving room," wrote Doyle the novelist, later in life, "with a face like a red Indian, and diagnose the people as they came in, before they even opened their mouths. He would tell them their symptoms, and even give them details of their past life; and hardly ever would he make a mistake."

The results were often highly dramatic. To a civilian patient, on one occasion, he observed: "Well, my man, you've served in the army."

"Aye, sir."

"Not long discharged?"

"No, sir."

"A Highland regiment?"

3

"Aye, sir."

"A non-com. officer?"

"Aye, sir."

"Stationed at Barbados?"

"Aye, sir."

"You see, gentlemen," explained the physician to his surrounding students and dressers, "the man was a respectful man but did not remove his hat. They do not in the army; but he would have learned civilian ways if he had been long discharged. He has an air of authority, and he is obviously Scottish. As to Barbados, his complaint is elephantiasis, which is West Indian and not British." [1]

And no little of the dry humor of Joseph Bell's deductions is visible in another case that is of record.

"What is the matter with this man, sir?" he inquired of a trembling student, standing by. "Come down, sir, and look at him. No, you mustn't touch him. Use your eyes, sir! Use your ears, use your brain, use your bump of perception, use your powers of deduction!"

The stammering student did his best: "Hip-joint disease, sir?"

"Hip-nothing!" retorted Bell disgustedly. "The man's limp is not from his hip but from his foot, or rather from his feet. Were you to observe closely you would note that there are slits—cut by a knife—in those parts of the shoes on which the pressure of the shoe is greatest against the foot. The man is suffering from corns, gentlemen, and has no hip trouble at all. But he has not come to us to be treated for corns, gentlemen; we are not chiropodists. His trouble is of a more serious nature. This is a case of chronic alcoholism, gentlemen. The rubicund nose, the puffed and bloated face, the bloodshot eyes, the tremulous hands and twitching face muscles, with the quick, pulsating temporal arteries, all combine to show us this. But these deductions, gentlemen, must be

[1] A. C. Doyle, *Memories and Adventures.*

confirmed by absolute and concrete evidence. In this instance, my diagnosis is confirmed by the neck of a whisky bottle protruding from the patient's right-hand pocket." [2]

Of another patient, he once said: "Gentlemen, we have here a man who is either a cork-cutter or a slater. If you will use your eyes a moment, you will be able to define a slight hardening—a regular callus, gentlemen—on one side of his forefinger, and a thickening on the outer side of the thumb; a sure sign that he follows the one occupation or the other." [3]

And of still another, he observed: "Gentlemen, a fisherman! You will note that, although it is a summer's day, and very hot, the patient is wearing top boots. When he sat upon the chair they were plainly visible. No one but a sailor would wear top boots at this season of the year. The shade of tan upon his face shows him to be coastwise, not a deep-sea sailor who makes foreign lands. His tan is that produced by one climate only—it is a local tan. A knife scabbard shows beneath his coat, the kind used by fishermen in this part of the world. He is concealing a quid of tobacco in the farthest corner of his mouth, and he manages it very adroitly indeed, gentlemen. The sum of these deductions is that he is a fisherman. Further to prove the correctness of my diagnosis, I notice a number of fish-scales adhering to his clothes and hands, while the odour of fish announced his arrival in a most marked and striking manner." [4]

To the wondering Watsons it was all very marvelous indeed.

Waiting and smoking in his sitting room at Southsea, young Dr. Conan Doyle heard again the strident voice of

[2] H. E. Jones, "The Original of Sherlock Holmes."

[3] *Ibid.*

[4] *Ibid.*

his former mentor, haranguing the awkward students of Edinburgh's school of medicine. In one familiar and oft-repeated apothegm there was the very substance of a new detective. . . .

> From close observation and deduction, gentlemen, it is possible to make a diagnosis that will be correct in any case. However, you must not neglect to ratify your deductions, to substantiate your diagnoses, with the stethoscope and by all other recognized and every-day methods.[5]

Out of his memories of Joseph Bell, hawk-faced and a trifle eerie for all his humor, the creator of Sherlock Holmes built the outlines of his great detective. But it was an outline only; it was the special genius of Conan Doyle himself that was to enable him to complete the picture. It was from the first, indeed, only the potentialities of a living Sherlock Holmes latent within his medical creator that made possible the gaunt detective's entrance upon the foggy stage of London's wickedness.

The name, one fancies, was an inspiration. To think of Sherlock Holmes by any other name is, paradoxically, unthinkable. It was a matter, apparently, that gave the author only slight concern. Obviously, his detective must not be "Mr. Sharps" or "Mr. Ferrets"; good taste rebelled against so elementary an epithet. His love for Oliver Wendell Holmes, the American essayist—also a physician—dictated the choice at one end: "Never," he later wrote, "have I so known and loved a man whom I had never seen." [6] But Sherlock was longer in coming. A leaf from a notebook of the period exists, and the astonished eye beholds it with dismay. "Sherrinford Holmes" was the detective's name as first it was jotted down by his

---

[5] Joseph Bell, "Mr. Sherlock Holmes."

[6] A. C. Doyle, *Through the Magic Door.*

THE GENESIS OF SHERLOCK HOLMES. A LEAF FROM
CONAN DOYLE'S NOTEBOOK

creator. And from the same source, one infers there was
an earlier name for Watson. The good doctor, one learns
with tardy apprehension, was to have been "Ormond
Sacker." [7] It is a revealing page, that page from Conan

---

[7] One of Conan Doyle's medical friends, a member of the Portsmouth Library and Scientific Society, was a Dr. James Watson,
who probably lent his name. This may account for the slip in
The Man with the Twisted Lip, in which at one point the doctor's
wife calls him James.

Doyle's old notebook, and a faintly distressing one. In the end, however, it was Sherlock Holmes,[8] and Sherlock Holmes it is today—the most familiar figure in modern English fiction; a name that has become a permanent part of the English language.

It was late in the year 1880, or perhaps early in 1881, that Holmes and Watson met and discovered their common need of the moment, which was a comfortable suite of rooms at a figure that would suit their pocketbooks. One inclines to the latter date, in view of the recorded fact that it was as late as March 4, 1881, that Holmes revealed his profession to his fellow lodger. Devotees will recall the passage in *A Study in Scarlet* in which the revelation is set forth; but one fancies that early readers of that first adventure came upon it much as Crusoe came upon the footprint in the sand.

Young Stamford introduced them, then vanished from the tale, his whole existence justified. The following day they inspected the rooms in Baker Street and took them on the spot.

It is amazing that the good doctor did not guess the truth about his new acquaintance weeks before he was told. Yet by that very failure to suspect he was forever to establish himself in the character of Watson. That first meeting, indeed, was to establish a tradition of the saga —a bit of dialogue which was, in essence, to be a sort of prologue to every tale that was to follow. The doctor's record of the line is precise:

"Dr. Watson, Mr. Sherlock Holmes," said Stamford, introducing us.

"How are you?" he said cordially, gripping my hand

---

[8] "Years ago," Conan Doyle was once quoted in a newspaper, "I made thirty runs against a bowler by the name of Sherlock, and I always had a kindly feeling for that name."

with a strength for which I should hardly have given him credit. "You have been in Afghanistan, I perceive."

"How on earth did you know that?" I asked in astonishment.

The Lauriston Gardens Mystery, it will be recalled, followed quickly on the heels of Holmes's confession that he was a consulting detective—perhaps the only one in the world; and for the first time, under the eyes of his admiring Boswell, the greatest detective of history or fiction set forth upon his mission of humane vengeance. It was a perfect morning for the adventure—that is, "it was a foggy, cloudy morning, and a dun-coloured veil hung over the house-tops, looking like the reflection of the mud-coloured streets beneath." And a man named Enoch Drebber, of Cleveland, U.S.A., or so his cards declared, was dead in dreadful circumstances, in a house at No. 3, *comma*, Lauriston Gardens, a little off the Brixton Road.

Thus opened the strange case of Jefferson Hope, for which Gregson and Lestrade, of Scotland Yard, received the credit, but which was solved by Mr. Sherlock Holmes of Baker Street, as later set forth by his friend and companion, Dr. John H. Watson, who had all the facts in his notes. It is an admirable bit of melodrama, well told in vigorous Anglo-Saxon English, delayed in the middle by a secondary story that is reminiscent of Bret Harte at his worst, and ending on the inevitable explanation of the detective. Doyle's first title for the book was *A Tangled Skein* but, happily, he changed his mind.

The book was written in the spring of 1886 and by July had been returned by Arrowsmith, unread. "Two or three others sniffed and turned away." The friendly editor of the *Cornhill Magazine*, who had paid £30 for a much shorter tale, found it at once too short and too long. On the point of laying it away beside its predecessor, *The Firm of Girdlestone*, the despairing author bethought himself of yet another publisher who might be cozened. Thus near was Sherlock Holmes to dying at his birth.

Ward, Lock & Company received the tattered manuscript and looked it over, and on the last day of October Dr. Conan Doyle, gloomily smoking in his patients' sitting room, received a letter.

Dear Sir—We have read your story and are pleased with it. We could not publish it this year as the market is flooded at present with cheap fiction, but if you do not object to its being held over till next year, we will give you £25 for the copyright.

It was not a tempting offer, even for so impecunious a practitioner as Dr. Conan Doyle. Sick at heart, however, with repeated disappointments, he wrote a letter of acceptance, and the deed was done; Sherlock Holmes was committed to the publishers, the pirates, and the world. *A Study in Scarlet* appeared in *Beeton's Christmas Annual* of 1887. At no time, the author tells us in his autobiography, did he receive another penny for it. Yet so often has it been reprinted and pirated and otherwise put forth, in many lands, that a very decent income might have been assured by that first slender volume— when later volumes had been written—if only its author might have retained his title.

That lurid paperback is today one of the rarest books of modern times—a keystone sought by discriminating collectors in every corner of the earth. Of equal rarity, and possibly even more difficult to find, is the second edition of the tale, with illustrations by the author's father, Charles Doyle. It was issued in 1888, with a brief publisher's preface that is a masterpiece of inept rhetoric and comparison. "The *Study in Scarlet* and the unravelling of the aparently unfathomable mystery by the cool shrewdness of Mr. Sherlock Holmes," the reader was informed, "yield nothing in point of sustained interest and gratified expectation to the best stories of the school that has produced 'Mr. Barnes of New York,' 'Shadowed by Three,' &c., &c."

The line drawings by the elder Doyle are amusing, viewed at this remove. One wonders what his son thought of them, even in 1888. But Dr. Conan Doyle's kindness of heart is perhaps attested by their inclusion.

British literature in the eighties had a considerable vogue in America, and much of it for a simple reason. No international copyright protection existed, and it was possible to publish works from abroad without payment of royalties. But publication, even under these unfavorable circumstances, had helped to make a number of reputations. Among the reputations thus established, in some degree, was that of Dr. Conan Doyle. In England *A Study in Scarlet* had received some favorable but unvociferous comment; in America it was no inconsiderable success. Thus it happened that, in 1889, when *Micah Clarke* had been praised by Andrew Lang and published to the world, to mark its author's versatility, there appeared in London an agent for the American house of Lippincott, with knowledge of that author's previous work.

At a dinner paid for by the American, there were present by invitation Oscar Wilde himself, a garrulous member of Parliament named Gill, and the still impecunious physician from Portsmouth. Wilde's conversation was a delight, [9] and as a result of the eventful evening the happy authors were commissioned to write a novel each for *Lippincott's Magazine*. Wilde's contribution was *The Picture of Dorian Gray*; Doyle's was *The*

---

[9] So much so that H. W. Bell believed it influenced some of the early pages of *The Sign of the Four*—notably in the description of Thaddeus Sholto's house and conversation, and in similar detail.

Sign of the Four, in which Sherlock Holmes, for the second time—under the eyes of Watson—went forth into the London fogs on a trail of violence and murder.

The adventure is dated September, 1888; and the tale appeared in the issue of *Lippincott's Magazine* for February, 1890. Are there any who, having read it, can now forget it? It is still perhaps the most vivid and the best of all the many tales that were to follow and far, far better than the one that had preceded it. Of course, "the day had been a dreary one, and a dense drizzly fog lay low upon the great city. Mud-coloured clouds drooped sadly over the muddy streets. Down the Strand the lamps were but misty splotches of diffused light which threw a feeble circular glimmer upon the slimy pavement."

And through this melancholy glamour, in a four-wheeler, drove Watson and Sherlock Holmes, with Mary Morstan by their side, to a rendezvous beside the third pillar of the Lyceum, and thence to Pondicherry Lodge and the horror of the Grinning Face.

It was Jones, this time, who took the credit—Athelney Jones, you will recall, of Scotland Yard—and for Watson, at the end of the trail, there was a wife. For Holmes there remained the bottle of cocaine that stood upon his shelf, toward which, when all was over, his long white hand was slowly reaching.

The book appeared in the autumn of 1890, under the imprint of Spencer Blackett, and was popular from the first. Today it, too, is rare and difficult to find. But the money it made for its author was insufficient for his needs, and Dr. Conan Doyle continued to practice medicine at Southsea. A second ambitious historical novel, meanwhile, had been written—the doctor's industry was incredible—and *The White Company* was all but ready to take its place beside the earlier *Micah Clarke*. That Sherlock Holmes would again appear between the covers of a book did not enter the author's mind, save perhaps as a happy possibility—when and if some other publisher, greatly daring, should solicit Watson for another reminiscence.

Dr. Conan Doyle, for all his mounting reputation, was a modest man, and still a man of medicine who wrote novels when his profession did not pay. In the latter days of 1890, indeed, he was contemplating a happy union of his two vocations.

As a specialist, it occurred to him, he would have leisure for his writing and perhaps command a greater flow of patients; wherefore, he would to Vienna go and study to be a specialist. The die was cast and, as the year drew to its close, Dr. and Mrs. Arthur Conan Doyle closed the doors of Bush Villa behind them for the last time. There is today, one hears, a tablet on the villa, and "Doyle House" is a place of tourist interest. As the birthplace, so to speak, of Sherlock Holmes, it should be marked, one thinks, by national decree.

With the spring, his work in Vienna completed, a new eye specialist tacked his plate over a door in Devonshire Place, not far from classical Harley Street, and a new chapter of adversity was begun. "Every morning," wrote Dr. Conan Doyle later in life, "I walked from my lodgings in Montague Place, reached my consulting-room at ten, and sat there until three or four, with never a ring to disturb my serenity."

It was a situation made to order for literary work. A number of popular monthlies had begun to make their appearance on the stands, among them the famous *Strand.* To the thoughtfully smoking doctor, it appeared that a serial might be an impediment in such a journal, but that a series of short tales, featuring a single individual who would appear throughout the series, might be the very ticket. And, happily, the individual was at hand. In the long hours of waiting, all unknowing where it was to lead him, Dr. Conan Doyle, eye specialist, of No. 2, Devonshire Place, began to write his series of short detective tales, now famous the world over as *The Adventures of Sherlock Holmes.*

This time Holmes was in the world to stay. That lean and sinewy figure was to become a symbol as familiar as the Nelson Monument and the Tower of London. A figure of incredible popularity, who exists in history more surely than the warriors and statesmen in whose time he lived and had his being. An illusion so real, as Father Ronald Knox has happily suggested, [10] that one might some day look about for him in Heaven, forgetting that he was only a character in a book.

[10] Ronald A. Knox, *Essays in Satire.*

SHERLOCK HOLMES, REPUTEDLY THE FIRST PORTRAIT DRAWN BY FREDERIC DORR STEELE FROM A PHOTOGRAPH OF WILLIAM GILLETTE; THIS RENDERING BEING A SLIGHT VARIANT FROM THE ORIGINAL DRAWN FOR *Collier's.*

2

THE

METHODS OF

SHERLOCK

HOLMES

To the earnest student of the Holmes saga it must be clear that the medical practice of Dr. Watson, after his marriage, was not excessive. For a time it was substantial and satisfactory; but at no time, apparently, was it so heavy that, at a call from Sherlock Holmes, it could not be dropped for a day or two, or turned over to an accommodating neighbor. Watson, himself, we may be sure, for all his felicity, thought often and with happiness of his days at Baker Street, when he was a figure in events of tempestuous moment; and if he wavered in the face of duty, there was always his wife to urge him to listen to the siren call of adventure. Anstruther, or another, she was always certain, would do his work for him. "You are so interested in Mr. Sherlock Holmes's cases," she used to say.

Precious little urging the good doctor ever needed. He could pack in half an hour, and there was always a convenient train from Paddington or Waterloo.

Watson, at the close of the grim adventure called *The Sign of the Four*, it will be remembered, had won the heart and hand of Mary Morstan, and the marriage must have followed almost immediately. There is, unfortunately, a confusion of dates at this point which scholars have striven to correct, without much success. It is certain that at the time of the first of the recorded *Adventures of Sherlock Holmes*—the curious reminiscence known as *A Scandal in Bohemia*—Holmes and the doctor had not seen each other for some months. Yet the adventure is dated quite precisely in March of the year 1888: it was on the night of the twentieth that Watson, returning from a professional visit, saw the spare figure of his friend "pass twice in dark silhouette against the blind," and was filled with an irresistible desire to look in upon him.

If Watson's memory of this evening is correct, obviously it was at fault when indirectly he dated the earlier adventure of *The Sign of the Four*—which immediately preceded his marriage—in the month of September, 1888. And still other adventures, recorded later in the series, only increase the confusion by their whimsical dating. A plausible explanation of the difficulty must be found either in the suggestion that Watson himself was confused about the date of his engagement and marriage, or in the perhaps more likely supposition that Dr. Conan Doyle was careless in the matter.[1]

Possibly it is unimportant. The pleasing fact is that a Mr. Greenhough Smith was editor of the *Strand Magazine* at just the proper moment and welcomed the further reminiscences of Dr. Watson with flattering enthusiasm. It was in the seventh number of that journal, dated July,

---

[1] "In short stories it has always seemed to me that so long as you produce your dramatic effect, accuracy of detail matters little," Conan Doyle once said. "I have never striven for it and have made some bad mistakes in consequence. What matter if I can hold my readers?"

1891, that the first of the series appeared, and by the time the last was published, in the Christmas issue of 1893, the name and fame of Sherlock Holmes were known around the world.

But on that night of March in 1888, for Holmes and Watson the curtain was just ringing up. The gaunt detective was glad to see his friend again, after their separation, although "his manner was not effusive." That he was at work on a problem had been evident to Watson even from the street. The shadow on the blind told the story: "He was pacing the room swiftly, eagerly, with his head sunk upon his chest, and his hands clasped behind him. He was at work again. He had risen from his drug-created dreams, and was hot upon the scent of some new problem."

The world recalls what that problem was. The surprising individual whose letter had preceded him, and who was to arrive at a quarter before eight, was punctual. His knock upon the door was loud and authoritative. His stature was not less than six feet, six inches. His dress was astounding in its barbaric opulence, and he must have been an astonishing figure, indeed, even in *fin de siècle* London. "Heavy bands of astrakhan were slashed across the sleeves and fronts of his double-breasted coat, while the deep blue cloak which was thrown over his shoulders was lined with flame-coloured silk, and secured at the neck with a brooch which consisted of a single flaming beryl." His boots, which extended halfway up his calves, were trimmed at the tops with rich brown fur; and to complete the Stevensonian melodrama of his appearance, he wore a black vizard mask across the upper part of his face, "extending down past the cheek-bones."

He had not spoken, however, before Holmes was aware that he was addressing Wilhelm Gottsreich Sigismond von Ormstein, Grand Duke of Cassel-Felstein and hereditary King of Bohemia.

17

In the singular adventure that followed the appearance of this royal apparition—"the comedy of the King's photograph," it has been called—Holmes rose to heights of admirable ingenuity, although in the end he failed. Defeated by a woman! It is the only defeat of its kind in the long history of that superb career; and to Holmes, thereafter, Irene Norton (*née* Adler), of dubious memory, was always *the* woman. But the King was satisfied; and Watson was to record thereafter, for the most part, only a brilliant sequence of successes.

It is just conceivable that implicit in this first "short adventure"—that is to say, in this first of Watson's reminiscences in the shorter form—we have all that is essentially important in the saga of Sherlock Holmes. Be that as it may, it is an excellent tale, with all the glamour of the others, plus an admirable sense of the rooms in Baker Street and a delightful glimpse of the two friends working in collaboration. Insofar as Watson himself, as narrator, is concerned, it contains much of what was later to become a favorite formula in his narrations. It is practically all on exhibition: the Baker Street prologue with mystifications by the detective; the references to other cases whose secrets may not at the moment be revealed; the statement of the problem about to present itself, and discussion of the insufficient evidence at hand; the arrival of the illustrious client, with further mystifications and an elaboration of the problem; the adventure itself, and finally the fascinating if anticlimatic explanations of the detective, illustrating the ease with which it all had been accomplished.

Others among the reminiscences are perhaps more rigid examples of the formula, which, after all, was just beginning to shape itself in *A Scandal in Bohemia*, but few are better stories. For good measure, there are vivid firsthand glimpses of Holmes's "amazing powers in the use of disguises," which in later tales are more often referred to than shown in operation. It may well be, indeed, that the narrative lacks only a corpse or two of being quite the best of all the adventures. But the great fathomer's debt to Poe is evident throughout. For all his earlier and perhaps ill-considered gibing at Dupin (in *A Study in Scarlet*), it is to be noted that in *A Scandal in Bohemia* Holmes was not above taking a leaf from the book of that "very inferior fellow." The incident of Watson's smoke-rocket and the false alarm of fire at Briony Lodge could only have been a happy memory of the duplicity of M. Dupin in *The Purloined Letter*. There was always a touch of professional jealousy in Holmes's character that even Watson could not gloss over.

In the twenty-three further reminiscences contributed to the *Strand* by Watson, through the agency of Conan Doyle, it is evident that a sort of intermittent partnership with Holmes had been resumed. The order of the adventures is not, however, chronological and further doubts are possible as to Watson's memory. The dating is irritatingly insufficient. While in the main the biographical narrative marches continuously, there are many backward glances, and it is obvious that a number of the problems are recollections of the days that preceded the doctor's marriage, when he and Holmes were still fellow lodgers in Baker Street. A chronological table of the adventures, accurately dated, is not possible, although the talents of a number of scholars have been directed toward the compilation of such a table—notably those of H. W. Bell, Thomas S. Blakeney, and Jay Finley Christ, who are not always in agreement.[2]

But what a record of achievement the tales reveal! What a picture they disclose of London at the century's

---

[2] More recently, Gavin Brend, William Baring-Gould, and Dr. Ernest Bloomfield Zeisler.

end! Is it too much to predict that social historians in the years to come are as likely to return to Watson as to the pedantic McCarthy or the admirable Escott? Of all the annalists of that curious time one must prefer the humble John H. Watson, with his chronicle of crime and detection and his swift, kaleidoscopic record of bowler hats and "kerridges," of bicycles and Turkish Baths, of green November fogs and baking August sunshines. Few telephones had been installed to complicate the business of life; when Holmes made haste he sent a telegram. In every doorway lurked the minions of the Yard. The picture is unforgettable and unique. "Baker Street," says S. C. Roberts, "remains for ever permeated with the Watsonian aura. The dim figures of the Baker Street Irregulars scuttle through the November gloom; the ghostly hansom drives away, bearing Holmes and Watson on an errand of mystery." [3]

Queer folk came to the rooms of Sherlock Holmes in Baker Street, and always they came when they were in trouble. It was a grim business that occupied the talents of the great detective. There was the dreadful case of Helen Stoner, recalled by Watson from an earlier year; the shocking adventure of *The Speckled Band;* and that gruesome business of *The Engineer's Thumb,* which marked the summer of 1889. And the hideous adventure of *The Cooper Beeches* that all but cost Miss Violet Hunter her life. One recalls the surprising episode of the managing director of the Franco-Midland Hardware Company, who knocked on his own door with his heels; and the alarming experience of *The Greek Interpreter,* a curious problem that was called to Holmes's attention by his brother Mycroft. The singular adventure of *The Red-Headed League,* to be sure, was pure comedy to begin with, but it ended in the capture of the criminal upon

[3] S. C. Roberts, *Doctor Watson.*

whom Inspector Athelney Jones would rather have clapped bracelets than any man in London.

Throughout all, the remarkable methods of Sherlock Holmes are admirably in evidence; they are, of course, the *raison d'être* of Watson's reminiscences. And they are, clearly enough, the principles and tenets of Dr. Joseph Bell of Edinburgh, expanded and dramatized, applied to specially selected cases of—for the most part —fantastic crime. In them one hears again the dry inflections of the Scottish doctor, laying down his broad rules of diagnosis. . . .

"Try to learn the features of a disease or injury, gentlemen, as precisely as you know the features, the gait, the tricks of manner of your most intimate friend. Him, even in a crowd, you can recognize at once. It may be a crowd of men dressed all alike, and each having his full complement of eyes, nose, hair and limbs. In every essential they resemble one another; only in trifles do they differ—and yet, by knowing these trifles well, you make your recognition of your diagnosis with ease. So it is with disease of mind or body or morals. Racial peculiarities, hereditary tricks of manner, accent, occupation or the want of it, education, environment of every kind, by their little trivial impressions gradually mould or carve the individual, and leave finger marks or chisel scores which the expert can detect. The great broad characteristics which at a glance can be recognized as indicative of heart disease or consumption, chronic drunkenness or long-continued loss of blood, are the common property of the veriest tryo in medicine, while to masters of their art there are myriads of signs eloquent and instructive, but which need the educated eye to discover. . . . The importance of the infinitely little is incalculable. Poison a well at Mecca with the cholera bacillus, and the holy water which the pilgrims carry off in bottles will infect a continent. The

21

rags of the victims of a plague will terrify every seaport in Christendom." [4]

These are the accents of Sherlock Holmes himself. It is amusing to recall, however, that Dr. Bell, pleased by the success of the detective for whom he sat as model, in later years suggested problems to Dr. Conan Doyle, which were not—as the author admits in his autobiography—very practical. But Bell's appreciation of Holmes was keen, and his own description of the detective is very adroit. "A shrewd, quick-sighted, inquisitive man, half doctor, half virtuoso, with plenty of spare time, a retentive memory, and perhaps with the best gift of all —the power of unloading the mind of all the burden of trying to remember unnecessary details."

Holmes looked upon himself, it is to be remembered, as a machine. When he does not suggest it himself, the excellent Watson—like a Greek chorus—does it for him. Thus at the outset of the *Adventures,* and then not for the first time, we are reminded that "all emotions . . . were abhorrent to his cold, precise, but admirably balanced mind. He was, I take it, the most perfect reasoning and observing machine that the world has seen." Deduction, of course, was his principal tool of office, and seldom was he at fault. Observation was a close and important second, but it was not always necessary for Holmes to *see* to understand. Pipe in mouth, with eyes half closed or shut, he could listen to a client's tale of mysterious horror and know the answer to the problem before the man had finished speaking. Whatever he might reveal to Watson, in advance of the ultimate revelation, reading the doctor's account of a recital in Baker Street one is always certain that Holmes, himself, is hot on the track. A particularly difficult case was sometimes a "three-pipe problem," after the client had departed;

[4] Joseph Bell, "Mr. Sherlock Holmes."

but with Holmes of all people difficulty was only a word in the dictionary.

The importance of tobacco in Holmes's way of life, incidentally, has been pointed out by students of the detective's methods. "He is," as Father Knox cheerfully admits, "one of the world's great smokers." [5] While occasionally he tossed a cigar case to Watson, he himself alternated between a pipe and cigarettes. The pipe was largely for his problems. In ordinary conversation, or when time was short, an occasional cigarette was sufficient. In nearly all the tales there is the pungent odor of tobacco smoke. The rooms in Baker Street must always have been full of it.

The drugs—cocaine and morphine—with which, during the early days of his association with Watson, he used to "stimulate" and "clarify" his mind, were seldom necessary during the *Adventures,* a reform for which Watson was, in large part, responsible.

The familiar Baker Street pose of lounging indifference, in a dressing gown, however, only masked the turnings of Holmes's restless mind. Bursts of almost demonic enterprise followed quickly, as a rule. In pursuit, he had amazing energy. Holmes at his utmost must have been a sight to strike the Scotland Yarders stiff with astonishment and dismay. Sometimes on hands and knees he traces a culprit's spoor across a sodden garden; and indoors, it is recorded, he often lay flat along the boards, with glass or measuring line to verify his suspicions in the flagrant minutiae of a room's disorder. But there is nothing self-conscious about a machine dedicated to vengeance and retribution. Enviable indeed was the humble role of John H. Watson, whose privilege it was to watch; while Gregson and the others sneered. . . .

Granted the opportunity, gentlemen—one might cry,

---

[5] Ronald A. Knox, *Essays in Satire.*

in paraphrase of Dr. Bell—of recovering a single day out of the irrecoverable past, how would you chose to spend that sorcerous gift? With Master Shakespeare in his tiring room? With Villon and his companions of the cockleshell? Riding with Rupert or barging it with Cleopatra up the Nile? Or would you choose to squander it on a chase with Sherlock Holmes, after a visit to the rooms in Baker Street?

The notorious taste of Sherlock Holmes for theatrical arrangement and dramatic effects has been a subject of frequent comment; and so, too, has been his flair for sardonic epigram. His theatricality is evident in nearly all of the adventures. It is his most human failing—his appreciation of applause. It is the actor playing to his audience when he cries: "Gentlemen, let me introduce you to the famous black pearl of the Borgias!" It is the admirable manipulator of third-act surprises who serves up the missing naval papers, under cover, as a breakfast dish. In the matter of epigram, he is at his best where a flavor of paradox is involved, and two examples— celebrated by Father Knox as specimens of the *Sherlockismus*—are famous. As both have been misquoted in that scholarly churchman's study, it may be well to re- state them from the Watsonian text. The first is a snatch of dialogue from *Silver Blaze*, the speakers being Sher- lock Holmes and Inspector Gregory:

> "Is there any other point to which you would wish to draw my attention?"
> "To the curious incident of the dog in the night- time."
> "The dog did nothing in the night-time."
> "That was the curious incident," remarked Sherlock Holmes.

The second, from *The Devil's Foot*, a later tale, is part

of a conversation between the detective and a famous lion-hunter:

> "You came down here to ask me whom I suspected. . . . You then went to the vicarage, waited outside it for some time, and finally returned to your cottage."
> "How do you know that?"
> "I followed you."
> "I saw no one."
> "That is what you may expect to see when I follow you."

From this latter episode it is clear that Holmes was not above a bit of boasting on occasion; but it was never empty braggadocio. He knew his powers very well, and such boasting as he indulged in was usually ironic. There is a flavor of Dumas in his occasional rodomontade, a savor of d'Artagnan, who also made no brags that he was not able and willing to follow with performance. And the always tacit contempt of the detective for Scotland Yard was similarly well grounded; his tolerant scorn of the professional operatives is part of the very substance of the legend. Yet there is a certain apparent modesty that accompanies his transactions. "My trifling experience," he calls his greatest triumphs, when he speaks of them to Watson. False modesty, perhaps? Yet not quite false, nor yet quite modest. It is again the artist speaking, half depreciating the applause he has so well deserved. . . . "The stage," says Watson, "lost a fine actor, even as science lost an acute reasoner, when he became a specialist in crime."

It is obvious, also, that business lost a remarkable organizer. The number of assistants in the detective's employ—or ready to join his forces on a moment's notice—is not at any time eplicitly set forth; but it must have been a large one. The ease and promptness with

25

which a fine acting company was assembled to play their parts outside Miss Adler's window in *A Scandal in Bohemia,* points clearly to a highly perfected organization. And it is notorious that a veritable horde of gamins was at his call. Smart youngsters, too. "The Baker Street Division of the Detective Police Force," Holmes whimsically calls the gang at its first appearance, in *A Study in Scarlet;* in *The Sign of the Four* its members are the "Baker Street Irregulars." There are glimpses of them, here and there, throughout the *Adventures,* although their leader—a certain Wiggins—would seem to have been supplanted by one Simpson. It was Simpson, at any rate, who watched the rooms of Henry Wood in Hudson Street some months after Watson's marriage.

But Dr. Conan Doyle, in time, was weary of inventing plots. With mounting fame, his need for ready cash had passed. His program was ambitious; it even threatened the supremacy of Scott, whether or not the doctor realized it. Curiously anesthetic to the glamour of his famous detective, without the faintest glimmer of a notion that he had created an immortal figure in literature and a living figure in the world, he determined that he and Holmes must part forever. The public clamor was still enormous; but Conan Doyle—that author resolutely told himself—had had enough: "I saw that I was in danger of having my hand forced, and of being entirely identified with what I regarded as a lower stratum of literary achievement." Thus his explanation, years later, when he came to write his memories. "Therefore, as a sign of my resolution, I determined to end the life of my hero."

Incredible resolution! "Murder most foul, as in the best it is, but this most foul, strange, and unnatural."

To Conan Doyle it was natural enough; it was, he felt, imperative. The idea, he confessed, was in his mind when he visited Switzerland and saw the falls of Reichenbach. . . . "A terrible place, and one that I thought would make a worthy tomb for poor Sherlock, even if I buried my banking account with him. So there I laid him, fully determined that he should stay there. . . ."

It is a dismaying chapter, come upon for the first time, that *Adventure of the Final Problem*. One suffers with poor Watson. "It is with a heavy heart," he says, "that I take up my pen to write these last words in which I shall ever record the singular gifts by which my friend Mr. Sherlock Holmes was distinguished." They had not seen each other in some time. The year was 1891, and Holmes persumably was in France, "engaged by the French Government upon a matter of supreme importance." It was with surprise, therefore, that the doctor saw his friend walk into his consulting room, and with consternation that he noted the detective's appearance. Sherlock Holmes was paler and more gaunt than Watson had ever seen him.

Small wonder, for he had just foiled the third of three murderous attempts upon his life, all made within a single afternoon. He was at grips, at last, with Professor Moriarty, that colossal genius of crime. It was inevitable that they should come together at the end; and that neither one should triumph. *Moriarty!* "He is the Napoleon of crime, Watson. He is the organizer of half that is evil and of nearly all that is undetected in this great city. . . . He sits motionless, like a spider in the centre of its web, but that web has a thousand radiations, and he knows well every quiver of each of them."

It was the evening of April 24; that memory, at least, was burned in Watson's brain.

There was a chance, however, that Moriarty would be taken, that all would still be well. And Watson's practice, fortunately, was quiet. He was able to accompany his friend to the Continent, whither it was certain Moriarty, if he escaped the net, would be drawn in search of them. The falls of Reichenbach were waiting their

WINDLESHAM,
CROWBOROUGH,
SUSSEX.

Dear Mr Vincent Starrett

It was really very kind of you to write so heartily about Holmes. My own feelings towards him are rather mixed for I feel that he has obscured a good deal of my more serious work, but that no doubt will right itself in time — or if not, it does not really matter. I am so busy with my history of the war, and see so clearly how many changes, additions &c will be needed, that I feel I have mortgaged the rest of my life, but really I could not have done so to a better cause. To drop a leaf of laurel on our dead boys would be the best topup to my life's work I could imagine

Yours sincerely   Arthur Doyle

SIR ARTHUR CONAN DOYLE'S COMMENT ON
SHERLOCK HOLMES IN A 1918 LETTER TO THE AUTHOR

arrival. . . . "A fearful place. . . . The long sweep of green water roaring for ever down, and the thick flickering curtain of spray hissing for ever upwards," turned Watson a bit giddy. "We stood near the edge," he says, "peering down at the gleam of the water breaking far below us against the black rocks, and listening to the half-human shout which came booming up with the spray out of the abyss." It was then the afternoon of May 4.

And then the false and fatal message—calling the doctor back! And Moriarty walking swiftly along the curving path that led upward to the brink! And Holmes's final letter written on pages torn from his notebook: "My dear Watson—I write these few lines through the courtesy of Mr. Moriarty, who awaits my convenience for the final discussion of those questions which lie between us. . . ."

God in Heaven! So they were dead, both of them— the great criminal and the immortal crime savant—deep down in the boiling depths, among the jagged rocks of Reichenbach. And Dr. Conan Doyle was free to turn his agile mind to worthier matters.

He was amazed, he tells us, at the concern expressed by the public. "You brute!" began one vigorous, tearful letter of remonstrance from a woman; and from all sides were heard the sounds of lamentation. It was as if a god had been destroyed by treachery. So children mourn, perhaps, when Santa Claus is murdered by their elders.

The first volume of the *Adventures*, dedicated to Dr. Joseph Bell, appeared in 1892, under the imprint of George Newnes. It contained the first dozen of the twenty-four episodes, beginning with *A Scandal in Bohemia* and closing with *The Adventure of the Copper Beeches*. The second group appeared in 1894, from the same publishing house, under a slightly different title, *The Memoirs of Sherlock Holmes,* and was found to be one short of the last dozen that had appeared in the *Strand.* The adventure known as *The Cardboard Box* was missing, the reason for omission being, it has been asserted, the author's chivalrous regret that he had allowed a woman's reputation to be smirched, a literary practice which he deplored. Whatever may have been the reason, the story was resurrected and given publication years later between the red covers of *His Last Bow,* where it occurs most unchronologically, to raise still further doubts concerning Watson's memory.

The two tall volumes known familiarly as the *Adventures* and the *Memoirs* are today of considerable rarity, and are—bibliographically speaking—of the utmost desirability. Their enormous popularity in their day is evidenced by the condition in which most of them turn up. In the final chapter of copies of the *Memoirs* it is not difficult to imagine the stain of tears among the thumbprints in the margins.

Thus it was; and it was to be many years before the public knew that Sherlock Holmes was still among the living—that he was not dead, and never *had* been dead. Even Dr. Conan Doyle himself did not know the glorious truth. For three long years even the devoted Watson did not know.

Good old Watson!

3

THE

RETURN OF

SHERLOCK

HOLMES

The late E. W. Hornung, creator of the celebrated
Raffles, and brother-in-law (it is interesting to reflect)
of Arthur Conan Doyle, once made a very witty remark
in the form of a very bad pun. "Though he might be
more humble," he observed, "there's no police like
Holmes."

The public thought so, too, and the protest that followed the supposed death of the detective in the steam-
ing caldron of Reichenbach was formidable. This was
no paper hero who had gone to his death in the pages
of a novel, but one of England's greatest living figures.
The lamentation was universal and it was sincere. It is
probable that the passing of no character in fiction since
Little Nell, in Dickens' *Old Curiosity Shop*, so wrought
upon the heart of England and America. But if the death
of Little Nell threw nations into mourning, it should in
fairness be recorded that it also wrung the heart of her
creator. Conan Doyle, it must be revealed, was made of

sterner stuff. . . . "I fear I was utterly callous, myself," he writes in his autobiography, "and only glad to have a chance of opening out into new fields of imagination, for the temptation of high prices made it difficult to get one's thoughts away from Holmes."

Happily, it was not only difficult; it was impossible. In spite of the success of such books as *Rodney Stone*, *Uncle Bernac*, and *The Tragedy of the Korosko*— admirable tales, all of them—it was Sherlock Holmes for whom the public clamored. That the great detective was dead in Switzerland, according to unimpeachable authority, made no difference, since—as it was shrewdly pointed out—there were still hundreds of his cases upon which Watson had not yet reported. They had been mentioned, time and again, in the existing chronicles. There was, for instance, the "singular tragedy of the Atkinson brothers at Trincomalee," about which the public mind had long been curious; and the "adventure of the Paradol Chamber," a suggestive hint of Watson's that had not been lost upon the public imagination. More recently, there had been the "singular affair of the aluminum crutch," the "adventure of Ricoletti of the club-foot and his abominable wife," the "question of the Netherlands-Sumatra Company," and other unrevealed problems in which Holmes presumably had triumphed greatly. The details of these and dozens of other cases were all in Watson's notebooks, he had himself asserted, and the public thought it had a right to them.

When Dr. Conan Doyle at length relented (as in time he did) it was not, however, one of the problems mentioned by Watson that he chose to present. It was the famous *Hound of the Baskervilles*, still perhaps the most celebrated of the many adventures of Sherlock Holmes. The immortal tale began its career in the pages of the *Strand* during 1901, and was in hard covers the following year. It was in this same year (1902) that Conan

Doyle received his knighthood from a grateful king and became Sir Arthur. Editorial gossip of the period had it that the honor was bestowed in recognition of his work in South Africa and for his history of the Boer War; but devotees of Sherlock Holmes knew better. It was a mark of royal gratitude for the return of Sherlock Holmes, and nothing else.

Our own gratitude must in part be given to B. Fletcher Robinson, the author's friend, for reasons which are set forth in the dedication to the printed volume. "My dear Robinson," the notice runs, "it was to your account of a West-country legend that this tale owes its inception. For this and for your help in the detail all thanks."

All thanks, indeed.

The story is a reminiscence of the year '89, it would appear, and again Watson's memory is rather desperately at fault. In the year '89, by his own earlier figures, he was a married man, only occasionally revisiting Baker Street. It is, of course, possible that his wife was away at the time of the adventure and that she conveniently remained away while it ran its course; but the theory will not hold much water. At no time does he mention Mrs. Watson (née Mary Morstan), whom traditionally he married some time in 1888. To the contrary, it is clear that he and Holmes were, at the time, fellow lodgers in Baker Street, without thought of change. From every indication, then, the problem of the Hound preceded Watson's romantic marriage and, therefore, preceded the adventure called *The Sign of the Four*.

In any case, it was one of Holmes's finest problems, and Watson—good fellow—has given it to us in full. It is the longest of his many reminiscences.

The story is too well known to need retelling. Who is there that has forgotten the dreadful death of Hugo Baskerville on the moor, and the foul unnatural thing

33

that stood above him? "A great black beast, shaped like a hound, yet larger than any hound that ever mortal eye rested upon." And even as the drunken roisterers who had followed recoiled from the spectacle, "the thing tore the throat out of Hugo Baskerville, on which, as it turned its blazing eyes and dripping jaws upon them, the three shrieked with fear and rode for dear life, still screaming, across the moor."

Two hundred years before, this thing had happened; and down the years the Baskervilles had perished, father and son, by means which had been at once "sudden, bloody, and mysterious." Was it conceivable that in the nineteenth century such things were possible? Yet now Sir Charles was dead in circumstances equally tragic and mysterious.

It was a sinister affair that Dr. James Mortimer laid before the great detective, that morning in Baker Street, and one that was to pit the fathomer against a foeman worthy of his steel. The public facts were simple. No indication of violence had been discovered on Sir Charles's person, unless it were an incredible distortion of the face. Before retiring he had gone for his evening walk and had not returned. In the Yew Alley where they found his body were evidences that he had paused beside a gate and looked out across the moor. Organic heart disease was sufficient explanation for the countryside. Such were the public facts. The private facts disclosed a singular circumstance which Barrymore, the butler, had neglected to relate on the witness stand. He had said there were no traces on the ground beside the body.

But Dr. Mortimer knew better . . . "some little distance off, but fresh and clear."

"Footprints?" asked Holmes.

"Footprints."

"A man's or a woman's?"

"Mr. Holmes," the doctor whispered, "they were *the footprints of a gigantic hound!*" [1]

Thus the problem opened, and that Sir Henry Baskerville did not follow Sir Charles to his ancestral door was due entirely to Sherlock Holmes and Dr. Watson Watson's part in the adventure is not lightly to be dismissed as unimportant. He was Holmes's surrogate at the beginning—on the scene before even the detective himself arrived; and there is Holmes's own testimony that it was an ugly and dangerous business upon which his deputy had been sent. Is there, one wonders, in all of history or fiction, an incident more thrillingly courageous than Watson's lone night charge into the empty hut on the moor? For all he knew, the murderer was lurking just inside. And in all of the adventures there is no more taut, suspenseful moment than that which follows —the moment when Watson, in a corner of the hut, hears the approaching footsteps of its occupant.

The perfect Holmes adventure, no doubt, would be a shrewd amalgam of the best parts of them all; such a tale would of necessity include many pages from *The Hound of the Baskervilles*.

The book appeared in March of 1902 and became a classic almost overnight. The enormous popularity of Holmes, however, dictated a large first printing of the volume; in consequence of which it is still possible, without too much difficulty or expense, to obtain a copy of the first edition.

But the tale was frankly from the notebooks of Dr. Watson—those capacious memorandums! It was a reminiscence of an earlier day. Poor Holmes, for all of Conan Doyle, now happily Sir Arthur, was dead and done for at the hands of Moriarty. The resurrection was a year away.

---

[1] In the original work these words are not italicized; they only *seem* to be. And that is the way many readers remember them.

To bring the dead to life is an achievement. And Doyle had killed his hero, in *The Final Problem*, with a finality that was appalling. Was he at all troubled in his mind about it? At the time of writing, not a whit. But it is impossible not to believe that, tardily, he felt regret. It is impossible not to feel certain that, in later years, after the murderous impulse of the moment had long passed, he wished it had been otherwise. At the very least, one can imagine him as thinking, he might have left the death of Holmes in doubt. There was Arabia to which he might have been sent, instead of Switzerland. Men disappeared for years in the Arabian Desert, then turned up safe and whole with manuscripts beneath their arms.

Yet the truth, when he established it, was as simple as falling off a porch. Holmes was not dead at all. Never for a minute had he been dead. Sir Arthur, like all the rest of us, had been mistaken; deceived by Watson's error at the brink; misled, no doubt, by Watson's later silences.

Watson himself had known since 1894, which was the year that "all London was interested, and the fashionable world dismayed, by the murder of the Honourable Ronald Adair, under most unusual and inexplicable circumstances." The crime was of considerable importance in itself, but it was its "inconceivable sequel" that lent it interest and importance to the doctor (who was by this time a widower, his wife having passed away some time during the years of Holmes's absence).

It was not to be supposed that after the passing of his two associates Watson would settle down with no further interest in crime; and we have his word for it that he did nothing of the sort. In point of fact, he never failed to read with care the various problems that came before the public; and more than once he even endeavored to employ the familiar methods of his mentor in their solution. For his personal satisfaction only, of course, and always—as he tells us—with indifferent success. The case of Ronald Adair, as it happened, had made a strong appeal to him—so much so that at six o'clock, one evening, he found himself one of a group of curious idlers staring up at a window in the dead man's house. Turning to leave the scene, he collided with an elderly deformed man and jostled a number of volumes from the man's hands.

There is no need to continue the account. The world has long since known the truth of that eventful meeting. The crippled bookman was Sherlock Holmes himself. And what more natural than his explanation, a little later, to the bewildered and delighted Watson? "My dear fellow . . . about that chasm. I had no serious difficulty in getting out of it, for the very simple reason that I was never in it."

Moriarty alone had fallen to his doom! "O frabjous day! Callooh! Callay!" One is not quoting Watson literally; but it is all there between the lines—his joy, his affection, and his satisfaction. And so once more Mr. Sherlock Holmes was free to devote his life to examining "those interesting little problems which the complex life of London so plentifully presents."

For sensible reasons he had sent not even Watson word of his survival. The trial of Moriarty's sinister gang had left two of its most dangerous members at large— criminals who would leave no stone unturned to bring about the death of Holmes, once it became known that he had returned to London. Silence, a long vacation, had seemed the wisest course. For two years he had traveled in Tibet, and for a time had conducted a laboratory at Montpellier, in France. Then the Park Lane Mystery had drawn him home—the murder of the Honourable Ronald Adair, which offered him peculiar personal opportunities. He was again in Baker Street, and all was as it ever had been and ever shall be.

The Return of Sherlock Holmes, a series of thirteen reminiscences in Watson's shorter manner, began to run in the *Strand* in October, 1903, and was concluded in the corresponding month of 1904. By February of 1905, the tales were in covers and another difficult volume had been added to the lists of bibliophilic desiderata. The reason for the book's rarity in its first edition form, in spite of a large printing, is obviously its tremendous popularity in its day. Less difficult to find than the earliest volumes of the series, it is much scarcer than *The Hound of the Baskervilles,* which was published three years before it. That is a phenomenon that can be explained only by the supposition that the short stories are, on the whole, even more popular than the novels.

Some of the most famous of the adventures are between the covers of that book, and some of Holmes's most skillful reasoning. Few better stories are to be found in the entire saga than those, in this sixth volume, known as *The Dancing Men, The Six Napoleons,* and *The Golden Pince-nez.* It is to be noted, however, how curiously many of Holmes's problems, in effect, repeat themselves, from first to last. It is almost as if, returning after his reputed death in Switzerland, he began the cycle over again—so much in common have *A Scandal in Bohemia* and *The Norwood Builder; The Blue Carbuncle* and *The Six Napoleons; The Greek Interpreter* and *The Solitary Cyclist; The Naval Treaty* and *The Second Stain.* And one suspects that the dangerous adventure of *The Dancing Men* followed with singular fortuity the detective's reading—or rereading—of Poe's *Gold Bug.* Not that it really matters. And, no doubt, it is merely further evidence in support of Holmes's own contention. "There is nothing new under the sun," he told Inspector Gregson, in *A Study in Scarlet,* adding significantly, "It has all been done before."

In spite of everything, London remained a fascinating

place. One cannot agree with Holmes that the loss of Professor Moriarty left it a "singularly uninteresting city." There was all the rest of criminal England to furnish him with problems. "From the years 1894 to 1901 inclusive, Mr. Sherlock Holmes was a very busy man," writes Watson authoritatively at the beginning of *The Solitary Cyclist.* Not only was he consulted in all public cases of importance, but he was called upon to handle hundreds of private cases, "some of them of the most intricate and extraordinary character." Among these, few perhaps were more sensational than that involving Charles Augustus Milverton, in which Holmes and Watson committed midnight burglary to serve the ends of justice; and certainly none was more highly colored with the hues of blood than that which saw the death of Captain Peter Carey—pinned to his cabin wall like a beetle on a card. The suggestion that Moriarty had left no competent successors was surely one of Holmes's most ironic jests. Throughout this period of prolific felony and misdemeanor, the old intimacy between the two friends prevailed. Many were the startling quests on which they ventured forth, in fog and sunshine, and all too few of them are recorded in print. The fact is, at the conclusion of the *Return,* Watson is again prepared to swear off writing—or furnishing materials to Conan Doyle.

It had been his intention, he tells us, to conclude his series with *The Adventure of the Abbey Grange,* an oddly twisted problem that came to the collaborators one frosty morning during the winter of '97; but the circumstances of an earlier promise to relate the puzzling *Adventure of the Second Stain* obtained from Holmes a final dispensation, and for readers of 1904 a final story. Holmes, it appears, had been for some time reluctant to see the reminiscences continue. We learn the reason with something of a shock. "So long as he was in actual professional practice the records of his successes were of some practical value to him; but since he has definitely retired from London and betaken himself to study and bee-farming on the Sussex Downs, notoriety has become hateful to him." Our shock is occasioned by these sudden tidings of the detective's retirement, just as we are congratulating ourselves on his return.

The date of publication at this point becomes important, however, for it enables us to establish the time of Holmes's retirement, without reference to Watson's notoriously faulty memory. It is a matter that has been a trifle cloudy; and Mr. S. C. Roberts [2] rather begs the issue when he loosely asserts that "by 1907 Holmes had definitely retired from professional work." In point of fact, Holmes had retired by December, 1904. It was in the issue of the *Strand* of that month and year that Watson's *Second Stain* reminiscence first appeared, with its clear-cut statement that the detective was even then keeping his bees on the Sussex Downs. Precisely how long before this Holmes had given over his practice it is only possible to guess; but it must have been a number of months, in view of Watson's reference to his friend's objections to the "continued publication" of his experiences.

Nevertheless, three further volumes of reminiscences were to follow. Of the first, *The Valley of Fear*,[3] published in 1914–15, it may be noted that it was one of Holmes's early cases, and that it shows up Watson's memory again. Since Moriarty is the off-stage villain of the piece, not yet precipitated into the Reichenbach, it is clear that the adventure belongs to a time before the tragedy of *The Final Problem*. Yet whereas Watson, in *The Final Problem*, declares his ignorance even of Mo-

---

[2] Later Sir Sidney.

[3] In John Dickson Carr's opinion the finest of all the tales.

riarty's name, in *The Valley of Fear* he speaks of him with familiarity. One often wonders that Holmes relied as much on Watson as he did. But the rarefied heights of Watson's unreliability in the matter of dates are better viewed from the opening paragraph of *Wisteria Lodge*, the first adventure in the volume known as *His Last Bow* (1917).

"I find it recorded in my notebook," he begins, "that it was a bleak and windy day towards the end of March in the year 1892. Holmes had received a telegram whilst we sat at lunch, and he had scribbled a reply. . . . Suddenly he turned upon me with a mischievous twinkle in his eyes."

But Holmes, my dear Watson, was dead beneath the falls of Reichenbach, on that bleak and windy day of March in 1892, at least you thought he was! It was May 4, 1891, that you bent above the brink and called his name. It was not until the spring of 1894, the year of Ronald Adair's inexplicable murder, that you met the crippled bookseller and found that he was Holmes.

But the answer is ready to our hand—even to Watson's hand. The reading is quite clear. . . . "I find it recorded in my notebook." We have seen before that not all that went into the doctor's notebooks was beyond a suspicion of inaccuracy. No doubt the year was 1902. If the matter is of further interest, it might be verified by a letter to the London minister for San Pedro.

For the rest—save only for the last—the tales are apparently Watsonian reminiscences of earlier days; one, *The Bruce-Partington Plans*, is dated 1895 and is one of the finest in the saga. Written at various times between the years 1908 and 1917, they were collected from the pages of the *Strand* and issued in covers in the latter year, the year of Sherlock Holmes's ultimate service to his country. In a preface, all too brief, we have from Watson's pen the last word that has come directly to us from Sussex Downs.

"The friends of Mr. Sherlock Holmes," he writes, "will be glad to learn that he is still alive and well, though somewhat crippled by occasional attacks of rheumatism"; and the detective's secret retreat is recklessly identified. He lives, it appears, "on a small farm upon the Downs, five miles from Eastbourne, where his time is divided between philosophy and agriculture."

Of Holmes's final service to his country, there is nothing new that needs to be said, except perhaps that—to American ears—his "Yankee" slang, throughout the adventure, is a little startling. It is as if he had just learned it all, and all at once, and was determined to omit no single word. And since, unhappily, the experience is narrated in the third person, by an unknown chronicler, no part of it may be specifically charged against Watson.

In this connection, and at this time, however, it should be said that there are scholars in the world who hold that Watson is to be charged with much more than simple inaccuracies of dating. He is the actual *inventor*, they assert, of certain of the adventures, which they declare to be spurious on grounds that are frequently well taken. There are even those who insist that the final volume of the series—a set of stories put forth as *The Case-Book of Sherlock Holmes* (1927)—is so far below the standard of most of the earlier tales as to make it highly suspect either as good Holmes or good Watson. It is a serious suggestion, and one with embarrassing possibilities when it is recalled that two, at least, of the later narratives are presumably from the pen of Holmes himself, and that upon the canonicity of these tales may hang no less a matter than the fact or false report of Watson's second marriage.

Perhaps the mind of Conan Doyle again grew weary. "I think, Sir," an old Cornish boatman once said to him, "that when Sherlock Holmes fell over that cliff, he may not have killed himself, but all the same he was never quite the same man afterwards."

Sir Arthur disagreed; and—for the most part—the rest of us are with him. Good, bad, or indifferent, one wishes there were stories yet to come. And why may not one hope? There is still that long row of yearbooks, which filled a shelf in Baker Street; and the dispatch cases filled with documents—"a perfect quarry for the student, not only of crime," says Watson, in *The Veiled Lodger*, but of the "social and official scandals of the late Victorian era." Conan Doyle is dead, to be sure, and Holmes has retired; but what of Watson?

At least let us hope there may be another attempt to destroy these damning documents; for if the outrage is repeated, we have Holmes's word to Watson, "the whole story concerning the politician, the lighthouse, and the trained cormorant will be given to the public."

A VARIANT RENDERING OF THE D. H. FRISTON
SKETCH OF HOLMES. FRISTON WAS THE FIRST
ILLUSTRATOR TO DEPICT HOLMES
(*A Study in Scarlet*, 1887).

4

NO.

221B

BAKER

STREET

Once upon a time—but this is not a fairy tale—a group of French schoolboys, for reasons having to do with scholarship or behavior, or something of the sort, reached the English capital on a sightseeing tour. Asked by the erudite guide in command of their charabanc what they would like to see first, they replied unanimously, with a great shout, that they would like to see the lodgings of Monsieur Sherlock Holmes in Baker Street. One hopes the learned guide was equal to the occasion.

A great many persons have felt that way about the city of London—that Baker Street should come before the Roman Wall and the Houses of Parliament. And a great many persons, during his lifetime, asked Conan Doyle to identify the house in Baker Street. "But that is a point which for excellent reasons," he observes in his autobiography, "I will not decide."

Has he not done so, in spite of himself?

Like the problem of what songs the sirens sang, and

what name Achilles assumed when he hid himself among women, the question, although puzzling, has not been beyond all conjecture. There is of course the address, which is explicitly set forth in the first sentence of the second chapter of *A Study in Scarlet;* but it is misleading, not to say deliberately inaccurate, as tourists have discovered. It would have been impossible, however, for Sir Arthur (or for Watson) so often to have described the famous rooms without betraying some clue to their location, and much speculation has been pleasurably wasted on the mystery.

"Sherlock Holmes lived on Baker Street, you will recall, hard by what is now Waterloo Station of the Underground, in that district of Georgian houses, with colorless brick fronts, little windows, iron handrails at the doors, and chimney-pots." Thus Harry Hansen, in the New York *World,* on the occasion of Sir Arthur's death. "And Baker Street," he continues, "is not very far from Piccadilly, the Strand, Trafalgar Square, and Whitehall, where the trade and politics of the seven seas were somehow unravelled and routed throughout the later nineteenth century. I myself have stood in Baker Street and surveyed a suppositious upper story, wondering whether Sherlock Holmes was standing beside the dark hangings of the windows, looking up and down for a hansom-cab with a suspicious driver. I have wondered just how Moriarty went about it to 'make the place safe,' as he called it, and pictured the streets bare of traffic and pedestrians, pervaded with a feeling of imminent danger."

But Mr. Hansen was content with the impression, as was the present writer when he roamed the length of Baker Street upon a day in drear November. There was, indeed, a house at 66 which satisfied one's occult sense of rightness; but the notion that it was the very place has long since passed, in the light of the surprising research of another quester. It required the genius of another sleuth, gifted as Holmes himself was gifted, to run his eye along the many pages of the record and find the hidden clue. Other searchers paused, then retired in confusion, when Dr. Briggs announced his solution.[1]

The clue is in that admirable adventure of *The Empty House,* first of the collection brought together in *The Return of Sherlock Holmes.* One recalls the circumstances, growing out of the murder of the Honourable Ronald Adair—how, after a circuitous journey through silent, menacing streets, through networks of mews (whose very existence to Watson was unknown), Holmes passed at length through a wooden gate into a deserted yard and opened the back door of the "Empty House." The description of the place is definite, almost precise. Dark as was the house within, Watson followed his companion down the long, straight hall until dimly he saw the murky fanlight over the front door. The window-panes were thick with dust; the room was only faintly illuminated by the lamplights of the street beyond. Then Holmes's lips were at the doctor's ear.

"Do you know where we are?" he whispered.

"Surely that is Baker Street," said the puzzled Watson, staring through the dusty window.

"Exactly. We are in Camden House, which stands opposite to our own old quarters."

Camden House!

Spending part of his summer vacation in London, now years ago, the late Dr. Gray Chandler Briggs of St. Louis, the well-known roentgenologist, mapped Baker Street from end to end—a labor of love. He had devoted no little of his medical leisure to a study of the Sacred Writings. One suspects they crossed the ocean with him. The *Return,* one fancies, was under his arm. And his Kodak

---

[1] It has been challenged in recent years, however, by several scholars.

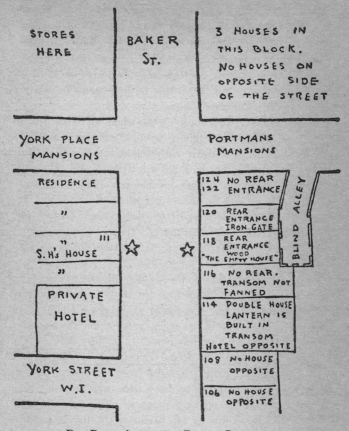

DR. BRIGGS'S MAP OF BAKER STREET

was in a convenient pocket. In the course of his investigations, he photographed the house at No. 111 and pronounced it that of Sherlock Holmes. No more brilliant identification, one ventures, has been made in our time.

Writing of his discovery to Frederic Dorr Steele, the doctor set forth the minutiae of his expedition. Like Holmes himself he had approached the empty dwelling from the rear. He had turned into a narrow alley and

47

passed through a wooden gate into a yard, to find himself at the rear door which had admitted the detective. Peering in, he saw the long, straight hall extending through the house to a front door of solid wood, above which was a fan-shaped transom. Conclusive all of it—for already over the front door he had read the surviving placard: *Camden House.*

"There is only one house on the whole of Baker Street that answers the description," wrote the St. Louis specialist, "and when I told Sir Arthur that the sign 'Camden House' was over the door, he was amazed. He told me, with such seriousness that I could not doubt him, that he did not believe he had ever been in Baker Street in his life; if he had, it had been many years before—so long that he had forgotten!" "There is something spooky about Doyle, anyway," added the doctor to his friend.[2]

The deduction that followed this discovery was, obviously, elementary. Since Camden House stood opposite the famous lodgings, the rooms of Sherlock Holmes in Baker Street were, of necessity, those upon the second story of the building numbered 111. One wonders if the doctor counted the steps. There were seventeen, it will be recalled, leading upward from the lower hall to the collaborators' sitting room. Watson was ragged a bit about them in the opening pages of *A Scandal in Bohemia.* But there was no bay window, Dr. Briggs noted, Watson to the contrary notwithstanding. That, he supported, was one of his confrere's little fictions.[3]

---

[2] F. D. Steele, "Sherlock Holmes."

[3] H. W. Bell, in *Sherlock Holmes and Dr. Watson*, takes serious issue with Dr. Briggs, pointing out that the northernmost stretches of the present Baker Street, including the building at 111, were, until January 1, 1921, known as York Place. Throughout the entire active career of Sherlock Holmes, he sets forth, the building at 111 was known as No. 30, York Place, a circumstance which he believes invalidates the doctor's identification, in spite of the strik-

For every reader there is, no doubt, a different picture of that famous living room, and probably it is not subject to change. Do you prefer it on a blazing day in August, such as that described by Watson, when Baker Street was like an oven and the glare of the sunlight upon the yellow brickwork of the house across the road was painful to the eye . . . a day when it was hard to believe these were the same walls which loomed so gloomily through the fogs of winter? On one such day, at least, with the blinds half-drawn, Holmes lay on the sofa and read a letter received in the morning post, which was to call him to the gruesome adventure of *The Cardboard Box*. But Watson's service in India, he tells us, had trained him to withstand the heat, and a thermometer at 90 was no hardship for that veteran campaigner.

Or do you like an evening in late September, when the equinoctial gales are raging with exceptional violence? Such days and nights brought tragic cases to the sitting room in Baker Street. What a picture, for example, is recorded by Watson in those early pages of *The Five Orange Pips*. . . .

All day the wind had screamed and the rain had beaten against the windows, so that even here in the heart of great hand-made London we were forced to raise our minds for the instant from the routine of life, and to recognize the presence of those great elemental forces which shriek at mankind through the bars of his civilization, like untamed beasts in a cage. As evening

---

ing clue offered by Camden House. But not necessarily, I think. York Place, it should be said, was a single block lying between Baker Street and Upper Baker Street and was an integral part of that thoroughfare. There have been Yorks this-and-that all over London since the Walcheren expedition made the dukedom immortal; but only one Baker Street known to cabmen. If Holmes or Watson had given his address to a cabbie as York Place, he would have had to add "Baker Street" to be understood.

drew in the storm grew louder and louder, and the wind cried and sobbed like a child in the chimney. Sherlock Holmes sat moodily at one side of the fireplace cross-indexing his records of crime, whilst I at the other was deep in one of Clark Russell's fine sea stories, until the howl of the gale from without seemed to blend with the text, and the splash of the rain to lengthen out into the long swash of the sea waves.

And then, the bell—inevitably the bell.

Looking from the window on such a night, which was a habit with both Holmes and Watson, one might have seen the occasional lamps gleaming on the expanse of muddy road and shining pavement, and perhaps "a single cab . . . splashing its way from the Oxford Street end" to deposit Inspector Stanley Hopkins on the detective's doorstep. And on such tempestuous evenings Holmes did not always attack his files with moody industry, or Watson lose himself at sea. There were times when they sat together in busy silence all evening, the detective perhaps "engaged with a powerful lens, deciphering the remains of the original inscription upon a palimpsest," and Watson "deep in a recent treatise upon surgery." Sooner or later, however, they were called away. It is at least astonishing, the number of cases that came to Holmes and Watson in inclement season, dragging them from their comfortable hearth to brave the rigors of indecent English weather.

Or will you have a cold morning in early spring, with thick fog rolling down between the lines of dun-colored houses, and the opposing windows looming "like dark, shapeless blurs through the heavy yellow wreaths"? The gas is lighted and shines upon the white tablecloth, upon the glimmer of china and metal, and upon Sherlock Holmes and Dr. Watson, at breakfast on either side of a cheery fire. Emerging from a cloud of newspapers, in which he has been reading the agony columns, the detective lights his long cherrywood pipe, with a glowing cinder from the coals, and lectures Watson upon the sensationalism of his records.

Not that they always breakfasted together. A schedule of their appearances at table would be valuable and interesting, but impossible. It all depended. That Holmes rose late is one of the soundest of our certainties—save, to be sure, on those occasions when he was up all night; but there were times when Watson breakfasted after Holmes. The record is surprisingly confused, and the only possible inference—as Father Knox points out—is that Watson breakfasted very late indeed. His own contention that he was regular in his habits has little bearing on the matter. He may have risen at noon and still have been quite regular. Certain it is that he resented early calls. Holmes, on the contrary, took what sleep he could and occasionally stayed in bed for days. But one likes to find them breakfasting together and wishes that it might have happened oftener. Rashers of bacon seem to have been a staple, with eggs, and always there was toast and coffee.

But attractive as is the picture of Holmes and Watson at their ease, it must be affirmed that it is a picture touched with confusion. Precisely where to place the chairs and tables, for example, the sofas and the shelves of books, and all the other dear impedimenta of the sitting room is something of a problem. Holmes, for all his orderly methods of thought, was notoriously untidy in some of his personal habits. One suspects that he moved things round to meet the exigencies of the moment and left them much as he had finished with them. One fancies Watson following in his wake and putting things to rights again. For the most part, however, the life of the detective went on around the fireplace. It follows that everything he might require would be within reach; certainly it would be so by evening on a day that he remained at home.

Not that Watson was conventional. "The rough-and-tumble work in Afghanistan," he tells us, "coming on top of a natural Bohemianism of disposition," had made him rather more lax than befitted a medical man. But there was a limit, even for Watson. "When I find a man," he asserts, "who keeps his cigars in the coal scuttle, his tobacco in the toe-end of a Persian slipper, and his unanswered correspondence transfixed by a jackknife into the very centre of his wooden mantelpiece, then I begin to give myself virtuous airs. I have always held, too," he added, "that pistol practice should distinctly be an open-air pastime; and when Holmes in one of his queer humours would sit in an arm-chair, with his hair-trigger and a hundred Boxer cartridges, and proceed to adorn the opposite wall with a patriotic V.R. done in bullet-pocks, I felt strongly that neither the atmosphere nor the appearance of our room was improved by it."

In these early paragraphs of *The Musgrave Ritual*, we have perhaps our most illuminating description of the room's untidiness. "Our chambers," Watson says, "were always full of chemicals and of criminal relics, which had a way of wandering into unlikely positions, and of turning up in the butter-dish, or in even less desirable places." It was his friend's papers, however, that principally distressed the doctor; they were all over the place. . . . "He had a horror of destroying documents, especially those which were connected with his past cases, and yet it was only once in every year or two that he would muster energy to docket and arrange them. . . . Thus month after month his papers accumulated, until every corner of the room was stacked with bundles of manuscripts which were on no account to be burned, and which could not be put away save by their owner."

There can be little doubt that Watson was a patient man. There were protests, now and then, no doubt, that have been omitted from the record. No doubt he rushed into the street when, as occasionally happened, the room became too malodorously a laboratory. The detective's chemical investigations went forward, it would appear, almost under the doctor's nose. Pictures of this side of his activity occur from time to time; a memorable one is afforded by the opening pages of *The Naval Treaty.*

A large curved retort was boiling furiously in the bluish flame of a Bunsen burner, and the distilled drops were condensing into a two-litre measure. . . . He dipped into this bottle or that, drawing out a few drops of each with his glass pipette, and finally brought a test-tube containing a solution over to the table. In his right hand he had a slip of litmus-paper.

It is another of those unforgettable vignettes of the detective and the doctor in their private lives. If the paper stayed blue, all was well. If it turned red, it meant "the life of a man." Holmes dipped the paper into the test-tube, and it flushed at once into a dull and dirty crimson. . . .

"I shall be at your service in one instant, Watson," he said, looking up from his labors. "You will find the tobacco in the Persian slipper."

It is one of the landmarks, that Persian slipper.[4] One fancies it hung upon the wall not too far from Holmes's armchair beside the fireplace. Opposite the detective's chair would be the doctor's—an armchair also, we are told—and it is unlikely that they ever swapped. Holmes's was low and worn, and broad enough to contain the coiled length of the detective in his moments of profoundest concentration. The rest of the chairs were scat-

---

[4] In a little-known poem by Robert Browning, "A Likeness," the poet describes a bachelor's apartment and notes "a satin shoe used for a cigar-case." Can this have been Holmes's inspiration?

tered anywhere, and three at least are indicated: a wooden chair, a cane-backed chair occasionally occupied by Watson, and a third armchair, presumably for guests. There was also a settee and, just possibly, a pair of sofas; or it may be that when Watson spoke of sofas he was thinking of a sofa and a settee. Certainly there was a lamp—in addition to the conventional gas fixtures of the period— and this would stand upon the principal table, beside the breakfast bell; and between the table and the hearth stretched the bearskin rug. Who can forget the extraordinary entrance of Dr. Thorneycroft Huxtable, M.A., Ph.D., etc., whose first action when the door had closed was to stagger against the table and collapse upon the hearthrug?

In a corner (when it was not in use) stood the acid-stained deal-top chemical table, with its accompanying stool. Was there also a bench, or was this bench or table according to the moment's whim? In another corner stood the violin case; and somewhere hung or stood a pipe-rack filled with pipes. The spirit case and gasogene were in the corner with the violin, probably on a shelf, one of the shelves, no doubt, that held the detective's books. Precisely where to put the desks down, though, is a puzzle. There were two of them, one Holmes's and one Watson's; and what with a safe still waiting to be placed, the room begins to be congested. Conceivably the safe was in the detective's bedroom.

The mantel, one gathers, was a mess. The clock stood there; and all of Holmes's unanswered correspondence, as we have seen, was transfixed in its center by the detective's knife. Presumably it held a medley of his souvenirs—and at all times a scatter of loose tobacco. Watson is clear on that point. Calling upon his friend, in the early pages of the Hatherley case, he found the fathomer smoking an early pipe while waiting breakfast —a "before-breakfast pipe," the doctor calls it, "which was composed of all the plugs and dottles left from his smokes of the day before, all carefully dried and collected on the corner of the mantelpiece."

On the walls one sees the scientific charts and such pictures as the friends found attractive. Two of Watson's are of record: a portrait of General Gordon, framed, and an unframed portrait of Henry Ward Beecher. Watson's opinion of the American clergyman was high, however, and probably this portrait also ultimately acquired a frame. The doctor's modest collection of books would require only a short shelf. His taste in literature was not notable. We may assume a medical group of some merit, with here and there "one of Clark Russell's fine sea stories," and a yellow-backed novel of the inexpensive sort.

The library of Sherlock Holmes, if one may so designate it, was personal and proprietary but decently eclectic. It would be a pleasant task to catalogue it for the record.[5] We are given many glimpses of Holmes's reading; it is a very respectable list of titles and authors in spite of Watson's early libel. A man who is able to compare Hafiz with Horace, to quote Tacitus and Thoreau, Jean Paul, Flaubert, and Goethe aptly and without hesitation, is not a man lightly to be called unread. Carlyle and Meredith too appear in the detective's reading—possibly they were on his shelves—and we may be sure of Winwood Reade. His reference works, including the *American Encyclopedia*, were numerous; they ranged from the current *Whitaker* to the Rev. J. G. Wood's *Out of Doors*. No doubt first on the shelves, however, stood the row of formidable scrapbooks which so many of his fellow citizens would have been happy to destroy.[6]

---

[5] This has been done several times by recent scholars.

[6] A collection of criminal cases brought together by Sir Arthur Conan Doyle was purchased by Dr. A. S. W. Rosenbach after the novelist's death.

There were two bedrooms, I think. About the doctor's we have the scantiest possible information: he comes from it, he goes into it, and there the record ends. Of Holmes's chamber there is a clear description. Since there was a blind, which Watson once was warned to let alone, there was perforce a window; it looked into the street (no other arrangement is possible in view of the statements in *The Mazarin Stone*). There was a bed and possibly a safe; and certainly there was a mantel, which suggests a fireplace. The mantel, like that in the sitting room, was a sight. "A litter of pipes, tobacco-pouches, syringes, pen-knives, revolver cartridges, and other *débris* was scattered over it." And every wall was papered with the portraits of celebrated criminals.

Three rooms comprised the suite. The arrangement, one thinks, was of the simplest: that is, the three were on a line, the famous sitting room between the bedrooms, and each looked into Baker Street. Inexpensive as they were, when Holmes and Watson first engaged them, it would appear that the rental advanced as time went on; but I like to think Holmes's generosity was as much responsible for this as any pressure brought by Mrs. Hudson. "The atmosphere of violence and danger which hung around him," as Watson says, made him as undesirable a tenant as could be found in London. Realizing this, it is possible that the detective increased the rental of his own volition. Certain it is that within a few years of his assuming occupancy—when, indeed, he was living alone in the rooms, Watson having married—his payments had become "princely." Watson had no doubt that the house could have been purchased for the sum Holmes paid for the rooms during the years they were together.

The point inevitably raises the question of the detective's profits, and the suggestion is that they were enormous. Yet in the face of this we have the assertion of

Holmes himself that he was a "poor man." The facts would seem to lie somewhere between the two extremes. "My professional charges are upon a fixed scale," Holmes told Gibson, the American Gold King, in *Thor Bridge*. "I do not vary them save when I remit them altogether." This was a dignified reproach, however, to a client he did not like. Fundamentally true as no doubt it was, it took no account of large rewards gained from more reputable endeavors. The truth is, one suspects, Holmes was somewhat of a Robin Hood; he took large sums when clients could afford it. And he balanced the account by handling many cases without any fee whatever. As to the rent he paid, what seemed princely to the humble Watson may, after all, have been no more than just.

Thus one sees the rooms in Baker Street, and somewhere on the premises a dressing gown. Inside the dressing gown is Sherlock Holmes. Watson too is there, as much a symbol as the immortal detective himself. That solid English figure—he was middle-sized and strongly built, with square jaw, thick neck, and moustache, according to a police description—must forever be the second figure in the immemorial picture; a man with qualities of heart and mind that command our love even when we smile at his absurdities. His independent virtues are not striking, but of the two collaborators he would be less trying on a desert island. It is through the eyes of this good, commonplace fellow that we behold the greater figure of his more celebrated companion, and his devotion to his friend in some degree is responsible for ours.

Thus they lived; and thus they still live—and the old street, at least, is there to prove it. It was no idle anecdote, that story of the charabanc of schoolboys.

And who is Sherlock Holmes? The spirit of a town and of a time. He is the fog, says William Bolitho,

221:B

Here dwell together still two men of note
Who never lived and so can never die;
How very near they seem, yet how remote
That age before the world went all awry.
But still the game's afoot for those with ears
Attuned to catch the distant view-halloo:
England is England yet, for all our fears—
Only those things the heart believes are true.

A yellow fog swirls past the window-pane
As night descends upon this fabled street;
A lonely hansom splashes through the rain,
The ghostly gas lamps fail at twenty feet.
Here, though the world explode, these two survive,
And it is always eighteen ninety-five.

VINCENT STARRETT

221. B

Here dwell together still two men of note
Who never lived and so can never die:
How very near they seem, yet how remote
That age before its world went all awry.
But still the game's afoot for those with ears
Attuned to catch the distant view-halloo:
England is England yet, for all our fears —
Only those things the heart believes are true.

A yellow fog swirls past the window-pane
As night descends upon this fabled street:
A lonely hansom splashes through the rain,
The ghostly gas lamps fail at twenty feet.
Here, though the world explode, these two survive,
And it is always eighteen ninety-five.

Vincent Starrett

in that crying old street, Baker Street; the glow of sea coal in the grates, where the English servant brings in to you tea and muffins, and snug napkins of odorous toast. He is ... the mystery of the house opposite; of the grubbly little shop around the corner you noticed and wondered about; of the old, old lady, half perceived in her shining brougham, who passes through empty Eaton Square every Wednesday afternoon. Sherlock is he who answers when you ask the air, Who lives there, I wonder? What is the story behind that drawn blind in London? ... From him you may expect something much too subtle to be advertised. Cabs slurring through the mud, sounds and sights and presences of the old nineties in Baker Street—that time and that place which above all thought itself final, and that nothing different was ever going to happen again.[7]

Michael Murphy notes: For those who know and revere Sherlock Holmes, his London address is familiar. Vincent Starrett's poem, "221-B," is the most famous verse ever written about Holmes and Watson. It is frequently read at the meetings of many of the BSI scion societies throughout the world. It has been recorded by Basil Rathbone and reprinted innumerable times.

My bibliographical reference indicates that the sonnet was first published in March of 1942 and dedicated to that eminent Sherlockian, Edgar Smith. If that is inaccurate, I am at least far from wrong when I say that this exquisite and telling poem has captured the spirit and flavor of 1895 with classic *vraisemblance*, and that it will endure as long as the adventures of the men it celebrates.

This reprinting of the poem is accompanied by a facsimile of Vincent Starrett's holograph manuscript.

---

[7] William Bolitho, "The Last Bow."

5

THE PRIVATE

LIFE OF

SHERLOCK

HOLMES

It is, of course, notorious—we have Watson's word for it—that Sherlock Holmes "loathed every form of society with his whole Bohemian soul." The word *society* has other connotations today. What Watson intended to convey was that *social life* offended the Bohemian soul of his companion; in consequence of which emotion Holmes preferred to spend his time in Baker Street when others might have gone to teas and parties: "buried among his old books," as Watson says, "and alternating from week to week between cocaine and ambition —the drowsiness of the drug and the fierce energy of his own keen nature."

In time, it is true, the doctor weaned him from the drug—to the detriment of romantic interest, whatever the benefit to Holmes—but even then it is seldom that one finds the austere detective accepting or turning down an invitation. He simply didn't get them. No doubt there had been plenty of them in his youth; but in the face of his consistent declinations—after an experience or two, perhaps with bores—he would in time, of course, be let severely alone. It is, one fancies, almost as great a nuisance to be a detective as to be a doctor; there are always guests with problems to present.

The fact is, Watson too preferred the silences or the friendly arguments of Baker Street to any attraction London had to offer—a circumstance in which he is at one with his adoring readers. Each man preferred the company of the other and was glad enough, no doubt, even to see a client leave the premises. Even, perhaps, Lestrade or Tobias Gregson. Even, perhaps, Inspector Stanley Hopkins; although, for Hopkins, Holmes had a considerable admiration, and on a cold night a prescription containing whiskey.

To the superficial student of the detective's cases it may appear that the rooms in Baker Street were always crowded. His first impression may be that of a bewildered client teetering on the rug; an armchair in which the detective is curled like a Mohammedan, smoking shag; a cane-backed chair or sofa supporting Watson; and Mrs. Hudson entering to announce Lestrade—whose footstep is on the stair. In actuality, there were long hours of comradely communion between the occupants. Seldom indeed did anyone stay the night. And surely some of the happiest memories of the epic history are those of Holmes and Watson living their simple, private lives. Not Crusoe and his admirable Friday were more resolutely at home upon their island than Sherlock Holmes and Watson in their living room. They passed there some of the most felicitous moments of their common life.

Not that they did not, on occasion, venture the Victorian whirl. There is ample record that Holmes, at least, was fond of opera—sufficiently so to hurry to Covent Garden, on a Wagner night, with no hope of arriving before the second act. This was after the successful culmination of the *Red Circle* adventure, and was possibly in the nature of a reward. Similarly, it will be remembered, after some weeks of severe work on the problem presented by Sir Henry Baskerville, the pair went off to hear the De Reszkes in *Les Huguenots*. Holmes had procured a box, and on the way they stopped at Marcini's for a little dinner. "Turning their thoughts into more pleasant channels," was the way in which Holmes described the De Reszke episode. A musician himself, he would naturally turn to music for rest and surcease, after a desperate morning round with murderers. Not always was his own violin sufficient.

As early in their association as the celebrated *Study in Scarlet* the detective had dragged his companion off to Halle's concert, after a triumphant morning of detection at Lauriston Gardens. Neruda was to play: "Her attack and her bowing are splendid," commented Sherlock Holmes. "What's that little thing of Chopin's she plays so magnificently?" [1] If he expected Watson to answer him, it might appear that the doctor knew something about music, which is doubtful. And luncheon, of course, immediately preceded Neruda. Both men, without being gluttons, were fond of eating, and frequently they posted off to some favorite London restaurant. After the hideous comedy of the *Dying Detective* it was to Simpson's they went for sustenance, however, not Marcini's. Possibly it seemed a better place to eat when food in quantity was required. Holmes, it will be recalled, had been at that time fasting for several days.

St. James's Hall was also a favorite sanctuary when it was possible for Holmes to interrupt his sleuthing. "And now, Doctor, we've done our work; it's time we had some play," one hears him cry to Watson, after a bril-

---

[1] It has been suggested that it was the Mazurka in E-flat minor, Op. 6, No. 4, transcribed for the violin in E minor.

liant morning of deduction. "A sandwich and a cup of coffee; then off to violin land, where all is sweetness and delicacy and harmony, and there are no red-headed clients to vex us with their conundrums." The occasion of this pleasant interlude was the intermission, as it were, before the "crash" in the fantastic problem of Mr. Jabez Wilson. And all that afternoon, the doctor tells us, "he sat in the stalls, wrapped in the most perfect happiness, gently waving his long thin fingers in time to the music —listening to Sarasate play the violin.

The picture galleries, too, it must be assumed, were browsing spots attractive to the collaborators. No doubt they served as stopgaps in the long days of criminal investigation—when it was possible pleasantly to while away an hour while waiting for an appointment. A clue to this diversion is to be found in the early pages of the *Hound*, after the profitable discovery of the bearded man, in Regent Street: "And now, Watson, it only remains for us to find out by wire the identity of the cabman . . . and then we will drop into one of the Bond Street picture-galleries and fill in the time until we are due at the hotel." But the incident was not, we may be sure, an isolated one. The mind turns easily at such times to the familiar groove. Did they, one wonders, care for Mr. Whistler? Or was "The Charge of the Scots Greys" more to their British taste?

It is clear, at any rate, that the occasional social exercises of the pair were largely cultural. When they went forth from Baker Street, it was upon a trail of evil import or to a place of decent entertainment. Occasionally, to a Turkish bath; and very likely—one suspects—now and again to Madame Tussaud's. On the whole, however, they preferred to stay at home. Away from it, the detective's temper was always uncertain, Watson tells us: "Without his scrapbooks, his chemicals, and his homely untidiness, he was an uncomfortable man."

From time to time they traveled on the Continent, not

always on the business of a client; and several parts of rural England knew them well. It was on one of these shared vacation jaunts that they chanced upon the ugly business of *The Reigate Squires*—when they were the guests of Colonel Hayter, down in Surrey; and it was presumably a holiday adventure of a sort that brought them the instructive problem of *The Three Students*— a sort of pendant to Holmes's laborious researches into early English charters. Again, it was a vacation trip that took them, in 1897, to the small cottage near Poldhu Bay, at the farthest extremity of the Cornish peninsula, in which singular and sinister neighborhood there befell that gruesome experience chronicled by Watson as *The Devil's Foot*. Once, it is certain, they went to Norway; but if aught of criminal interest developed during the visit, it has yet to be reported.

From these vacation trips—interrupted as they invariably were by theft or murder—Holmes always returned to Baker Street refreshed. It was, however, only the thefts and murders that consoled him for the time thus spent away from home.

And it is at home, in Baker Street, that one likes best to think of them, alone and puttering with their secret satisfactions. Little vignettes of perfect happiness, wreathed in tobacco smoke and London fog.

Of course they took in all the daily papers and read them with a diligence almost incredible. Did the detective prop his journal against the breakfast sugar bowl? Did Watson, when he sat down at table, invariably thump his knee against the leg? For Watson, at any rate, Holmes usually had a lecture. . . .

After his return from Switzerland, by way of Lhassa, the papers rather disappointed Holmes. With Moriarty dead, London, from the point of view of the criminal expert, he said, had become a singularly uninteresting city. . . . "With that man in the field one's morning paper presented infinite possibilities. Often it was only the smallest trace, Watson, the faintest indication, and yet it was enough to tell me that the great malignant brain was there, as the gentlest tremors of the edges of the web remind one of the foul spider which lurks in the centre. Petty thefts, wanton assaults, purposeless outrage—to the man who held the clue all could be worked into one connected whole. To the scientific student of the higher criminal world no capital of Europe offered the advantages which London then possessed. But now——!"

One sees the pile of papers growing in a corner, mounting up toward the gasogene and pipe-rack, till in a fit of energy Holmes scissored them for his scrapbooks. That rid the room of papers, for the nonce, but presented anew the problem of the clippings: there were probably thousands waiting to be pasted up. And then, another night, another burst of energy, and some hundreds would at length be docketed. Over the years the row of scrapbooks lengthened on the shelf. Cold winter evenings or rainy nights of autumn were likely to be dedicated to the pasting-up, sometimes to indexing what already had been done. A never-ending chore. When and if the British Museum ever shall acquire the scrapbooks of Mr. Sherlock Holmes, one hopes to read the volume under "V"—a fascinating miscellany. The *Voyage of the "Gloria Scott"* is there; a biography of Victor Lynch, the forger; the case of "Vanderbilt and the Yeggman" —unchronicled by Watson; and somewhat concerning "Vittoria the Circus Belle." *Vigor, the Hammersmith Wonder* is there too; a note on Vipers; and a Draculian paper about Vampires. . . .

Holmes obviously had a system of his own. Most scrapebook-makers would be content to index *Lynch* under the letter "L," and let it go at that. But Sherlock Holmes indexed his clippings to the last adjective and adverb.

The relationship between the friends was ideal, after the years had taught them to know each other. About his own share in the partnership Watson had no illusions; but he was not servile. Thousands of his readers, as he must have known, would happily have traded places with him. His statement candidly prefixed to the adventure of *The Creeping Man* is admirably lucid and not a little penetrating:

> The relations between us were peculiar. He was a man of habits, narrow and concentrated habits, and I had become one of them. As an institution I was like the violin, the shag tobacco, the old black pipe, the index books, and others perhaps less excusable. When it was a case of active work and a comrade was needed upon whose nerve he could place some reliance, my role was obvious. But apart from this I had uses. I was a whetstone for his mind, I stimulated him. He liked to think aloud in my presence. His remarks could hardly be said to be made to me—many of them would have been as appropriately addressed to his bedstead—but none the less, having formed the habit, it had become in some way helpful that I should register and interject. If I irritated him by a certain methodical slowness in my mentality, that irritation served only to make his own flame-like intuitions and impressions flash up the more vividly and swiftly. Such was my humble rôle in our alliance.

During the day, when no active occupation offered, Holmes smoked his pipe and meditated. With a case on hand, he also smoked and meditated. Sometimes—the picture is famous—he would sit for hours "curled up in the recesses of his shabby chair." Sometimes, in quest of information, he "sat upon the floor like some strange Buddha, with crossed legs, the huge books all around him, and one open upon his knees." Obviously, the nature of the problem offered for his solution had an important bearing on his habits. Sometimes "a formidable array of bottles and test-tubes, with the pungent cleanly smell of hydrochloric acid" informed the doctor— hastening in after a session with his patients—that he had "spent his day in the chemical work which was so dear to him." Sometimes, horizontal upon a couch, wrapped in a purple gown, "a pipe-rack within his reach upon the right, and a pile of crumpled morning papers . . . near at hand," the doctor would discover him in rapt examination of a strange hat that was for the moment an intellectual problem.

There is fascination even in the most trivial exchanges between the two, a sense of significance, of impending revelation, not always justified by the detective's disclosure. It is part of Watson's charm that he sets down everything; one would not have it otherwise. The little triumphs that are no part or parcel of the tale are his habitual prolegomena; they are almost our favorite glimpses of their private life together, those intimate moments when only the reader's eye may spy upon them.

"Sherlock Holmes," one thrills to read, and read again, "had been bending for a long time over a low-power microscope. Now he straightened himself up and looked around at me in triumph. 'It is glue, Watson,' said he. 'Unquestionably it is glue. Have a look at these scattered objects in the field!' "

Actively engaged upon a malodorous bit of brewing, "his long, thin back curved over a chemical vessel," his head sunk upon his chest, the detective looked to Watson like "a strange, lank bird, with dull grey plumage and a black top-knot." But this would be, of course, upon a day when Holmes had put on his dressing gown of gray, instead of the more familiar purple horror.

On the whole, the picture Watson had conveyed most vividly is that of Holmes recumbent—languid yet alert and dangerous in his chair, wreathed in the vapors from his favorite pipe. That favorite pipe, of course, was subject always to change; since nothing, as Holmes himself remarked, has more individuality than a pipe, "save perhaps watches and bootlaces." For every mood in Baker Street there was a pipe. One sees him still as Watson described him in one of the last of the published adventures. . . . "Holmes lay with his gaunt figure stretched in his deep chair, his pipe curling forth slow wreaths of acrid tobacco, while his eyelids drooped over his eyes so lazily that he might almost have been asleep were it not that at any halt or questionable passage of my narrative they half lifted, and two grey eyes, as bright and keen as rapiers, transfixed me with their searching glance."

One notes that Holmes's eyes were gray. Watson tells us so on five separate occasions.

Occasionally, when the day was fine, the friends walked in the streets, savoring the sights and sounds of London. Shop windows were of interest to them both, and passers-by absorbing. "The park" was close at hand; it is of record that they sometimes strolled there. Watson's account of one such episide is subdued. . . . "The first faint shoots of green were breaking out upon the elms, and the sticky spearheads of the chestnuts were just beginning to burst into their five-fold leaves. For two hours we rambled about together, in silence for the most part, as befits two men who know each other intimately." But this diversion was not customary, since it encroached on office hours. "There had been a gentleman asking for them."

"Holmes glanced reproachfully at me," confesses Watson. " 'So much for afternoon walks!' said he."

Afternoons, then, were spent in running down their cases—the detective's cases—not often in strolling in the park. And for all his love of Baker Street, it should be noted, during the active progress of a case Holmes was quite capable of hiding out. It is an interesting revelation, frequently overlooked, that Watson makes in his account of the adventure called *Black Peter*. . . . "He had at least five small refuges in different parts of London in which he was able to change his personality." The reference is tantalizing and obscure. The rooms of Mycroft Holmes, opposite the Diogenes Club, would certainly be one of them; but it would be satisfying to know the others. At such times—when he was operating in disguise—Holmes sometimes took the name of "Captain Basil," a precaution that gave Watson some uneasy moments; and there were other pseudonyms. It may be assumed that in all of his five refuges he stored the materials of deception, as well as quantities of shag tobacco.

Not all of the detective's cases, however, drove him to his retreats or to his armchair. Sometimes for hours —once, certainly, for a whole day—he rambled about the living room with knotted brows, his head on his breast, charging and recharging his strongest pipe, deaf to all of Watson's questionings. These were his bad days, when the trail was faint and even Watson had failed him as a whetstone.

But it was to the papers that both invariably returned. The everlasting, never-ending papers. Edition after edition was delivered at the rooms, probably by the stout and puffing Mrs. Hudson, who would have them from the urchin at the door. Not only Holmes but Watson saturated himself with the unending chronicle of news; and they read it—it must be admitted—with a surprisingly reckless acceptance of its accuracy.

It is at night one likes them best perhaps, these curious companions. And preferably with a beating rain outside. If Stanley Hopkins has dropped in from Scotland Yard, no matter; their simple hospitality is as hearty as it is restrained and masculine. They did not always save the whiskey for Stanley Hopkins. Occasionally, good fellows, they tippled companionably themselves. And usually in the early morning hours, after a trying day with thug or cracksman. Whiskey-and-soda and a bit of lemon—and all the credit gone to Scotland Yard! Midnight or very early in the morning—the time of relaxation and revelation—while the "undying flame" leaps on the hearth. Holmes lifts out a glowing cinder with the tongs; lights the long pipe of amicable disputation. "You see, Watson," he patiently begins, "it was all perfectly obvious from the beginning. . . ."

In the long evenings, too, Holmes played his fiddle. Probably his bowing was not comparable to Neruda's, but it was good enough for Watson. "Sometimes the chords were sonorous and melancholy. Occasionally they were fantastic and cheerful." "Clearly they reflected the thoughts which possessed him, but whether the music aided those thoughts, or whether the playing was simply the result of a whim or fancy," was more than Watson could tell. And when some haunting strain had charmed and soothed the doctor, moved him to ask the name of the composer, as like as not it was something by Sherlock Holmes.

Then, of an evening in the depths of February, one fancies Watson questing another tale. Permission perhaps to reveal an untold adventure, one of the many hinted at and then withheld. The truth perhaps about the atrocious conduct of Colonel Upwood or the peculiar persecution of John Vincent Harden. It is understandable that some reticence must be observed about the sudden death of Cardinal Tosca—which was investigated at the personal request of His Holiness, the Pope—and about that delicate matter arranged by Holmes for the reigning family of Holland; but surely, thinks Watson, the time must be at hand for a full disclosure of the facts in the Tankerville Club scandal. There can be no doubt that he often spoke of these matters to Holmes. Having half promised his readers that some day he would

71

tell those stories, his position may well have seemed to him embarrassing.

One sympathizes with Watson. Too long has the world awaited the adventure of the Amateur Mendicant Society, "which held a luxurious club in the lower vault of a furniture warehouse," and the little problem of the Grosvenor Square Furniture Van. The case of Wilson, the Notorious Canary-Trainer, too, is a whisper full of fascinating suggestion; and one would give much to read the long-suppressed "Adventure of the Tired Captain."

Holmes, we may be sure, listened to some urgent argument on those evenings when the doctor remembered his reading public. Sometimes the detective chided the narrator for his literary shortcomings, pretending that the tales were sad affairs; but when Holmes came to write just two of them himself he changed his tune.

One imagines them in whimsical discussion of the "ifs" of their adventures—the "what ifs," as it were, conducted post mortem on their cases. As, for example, that rocket-throwing episode in the amusing comedy of Irene Adler. It is impossible to read that story without wondering what would have happened if the ingenious smoke-rocket had missed fire. Would not the whole planned sequence have gone wrong? But Watson, although he may have faltered, never really blundered. Holmes knew the qualities of his assistant. No case was ever lost by Watson's failure. And his reward—all that he asked or cared for—was an approving word or nod from Holmes. Did he not get them both, outside the record? During those quiet nights in Baker Street after the problem had been solved forever—after the reader had put down the book?

How many matters of absorbing interest must then have been revealed! By means most dexterously disingenuous Holmes managed a glimpse of Godfrey Staunton's telegram on the first attempt. Yet he had seven different schemes, he told the doctor, if one had failed. What were the other six?

How many questions also must have gone unanswered. Holmes at times was blood brother to the Sphinx. There is a bit of dialogue that is in nearly all the tales. "You have a clue?" asks Watson eagerly. The answer is immortal: "It is a capital mistake, my dear Watson, to theorize before one has the facts." If one were called upon to find in literature the best inscription for a tombstone, it would be Holmes's cautious apophthegm. Watson should bargain for it on his grave. For Holmes's tombstone—"Elementary!"

But there can be no grave for Sherlock Holmes or Doctor Watson. . . . Shall they not always live in Baker Street? Are they not there this moment, as one writes? . . . Outside, the hansoms rattle through the rain, and Moriarty plans his latest devilry. Within, the sea coal flames upon the hearth and Holmes and Watson take their well-won ease. . . . So they still live for all that love them well: in a romantic chamber of the heart, in a nostalgic country of the mind, where it is always 1895.

6

THE SINGULAR

ADVENTURES

OF MARTHA

HUDSON

*Mrs. Hudson, the landlady of Sherlock
Holmes, was a long suffering
woman.*—"THE DYING DETECTIVE"

It rained in London through the night of March 3, 1881;
by morning of the next day, the streets were sloppy and
depressing. Some fog was abroad, and "a dun-colored
veil hung over the house-tops, looking like the reflection
of the mud-colored streets beneath." An Acherontic
sort of morning, all in all, and to Mrs. Hudson, standing
at her window at No. 221B Baker Street, it may well
have seemed that something harrowing and revelatory
was about to happen, or indeed was in the act of happening all round her. That disturbing consciousness of
singular events in prospect and proximity! For some
weeks now she had been mildly wondering about her
curious lodgers, in particular the tall one, with the thin

74

hawksbill of a nose and eyes set close together in a high domed head.

Conceivably, she only shrugged, observing that the day was cloudy, and turned her attention to something in the oven. But if the mood of doubt existed it must have deepened by the morning of the fifth. By that time the impending drama had begun to run its course. Used as she was becoming to the nondescript individuals who visited Mr. Sherlock Holmes, she had not until that morning set eyes upon the Baker Street division of the detective police force, and the sudden intrusion of a half-dozen disreputable street arabs must have given the good woman pause. Their pattering footsteps on the stairs were accompanied by audible expression of her disgust. What thoughts, one wonders, did she at that moment entertain about her principal lodger?

Thereafter came Gregson, of the Yard, taking the long flight three steps at a time—after almost pulling out the doorbell—and at his heels the sallow, rat-faced Lestrade, his garments untidy and disarranged. And then, immediately, the singular request of Dr. Watson for the sick terrier. To Martha Hudson, below stairs, it must have seemed that odd events were taking place in the chamber overhead. One fancies her at that moment, plump and puzzled, standing beside the stair-foot. Her dark brows are drawn in a frown, as she cocks her best ear upward. She is bending forward, her hands upon her hips. Does she catch a fragment of the conversation? Perhaps the strident voice of Sherlock Holmes, pausing in his eternal tramping up and down the room?

"There will be no more murders!"

Then, as she waits and listens, again the doorbell rings. It is young Wiggins, the leader of the ragged urchins, come with a missing cabman. Each in his turn mounts upward, and the door of destiny closes behind them. At the stair-foot Martha Hudson sniffs and turns away, then stops, appalled.

From the room above, a crash has sounded that seems to shake the building. Feet pound upon the floor and cries of fury filter through the ceiling. A desperate struggle is in progress, marked by every evidence of violence. And Martha Hudson, cowering against her doorframe, listens to the deadly scuffle with consternation and dismay. Her blood has turned to water, and she is weak with terror; yet in her bewildered mind she checks the values of furnishings now crashing to the floor, against the possibilities of their replacement by the villains responsible.

Ought she to send for the police? Yet Gregson and Lestrade were of the police, as possibly she may have known. One views her there, on that morning—frightened, indignant, with heaving bosom and disordered mind, waiting for the final, unpredictable catastrophe. An obscure, heroic figure on the outer rim of terrifying drama. Good soul, her direct secret fears at length have been realized. She had always known that something terrible would happen with that man in the house! And mingled perhaps with her alarm there is a little sense of satisfaction, of fearful triumph, that her predictions have been fulfilled.

In some such fashion, at any rate, must Mrs. Hudson, housekeeper to Sherlock Holmes and Dr. Watson, have come to a clear knowledge of her principal lodger's profession. There is no record that she was ever told, and, if she was, she can have had—until that terrific episode —no notion of what the simple disclosure portended. Watson himself had been informed only the day before. One hopes that Holmes, on his way downstairs with the prisoner, a little later, stopped long enough to allay their housekeeper's natural fears; and it is likely that he did, since he and Watson were permitted to remain upon the premises. There can be little doubt that Holmes made good the damage wrought by Jefferson Hope.

In this first instance of the dangerous nature of the

detective's employment, as it touched her own existence, Mrs. Hudson may well have sensed a chapter of adventures that would have frightened an ordinary woman into another line of business. It is perhaps a permissible deduction that already for some years she had been letting out her rooms to curious tenants, and was not unacquainted with the difficulties of the London landlady. However that may be, it has long been certain that she was not an ordinary woman. A young widow—one imagines her to have been—who took up commercial housekeeping when the episode of marriage was in some way tragically ended. But no whisper of her life before that day in 1881, when Holmes first called upon her, has ever been revealed. The notion persists that she had been unhappy; she kept so very still about it all.

That first occasion taught her, we may suppose, what she might expect of Sherlock Holmes. Yet some time was to elapse, one thinks, before he actually ventured upon revolver practice in his living room—decorating the wall with "a patriotic V.R. done in bullet-pocks"—and it is probable that this diversion was not frequent. A certain rapport would seem to be indicated between the two before such queerish pastimes could be tolerated, an understanding based on faith and works—at least, a feeling of certainty on the part of Martha Hudson that her curious lodger was able and willing to pay for a new wall, if necessary. Other and various scenes of violence and disorder must have occurred to prepare her for that first patriotic fusillade; yet even so it must have come upon her with a sense of shock. Loud voices, heavy falls, the crash of glass and table furnishings, even the noisome odors of experiments usually conducted in a laboratory—such matters may become in time part of the casual daily routine of existence; but shooting is always a little dangerous and startling.

One faintly wonders about the living room wall. That it was a substantial piece of building is rather certain:

77

solid beams of oak, perhaps, under a paper about whose pattern, save for Holmes's shooting, Watson has chosen to be reticent. It seems unlikely, however, that Holmes, a man of an original turn of mind, confined himself to a single set of initials, however appropriate. There were other monograms, no doubt, which Watson simply failed to mention. Mrs. Hudson, we may be sure, mentioned them on numerous occasions before the rattle of her lodger's patriotic gunfire became familiar.

But in time she probably told herself—and others—that nothing that Mr. Holmes now could do would ever surprise her. After the first episode of the Boxer cartridges there can be little doubt that she was prepared for anything. And one fancies that she came in time to like the perilous uncertainty of her position. There are persons who live with equanimity upon the slopes of a volcano, enjoying the threat of danger that hangs over them. After an eruption they return and build their homes anew, upon the very spot from which they were dislodged. So, possibly, it was with Mrs. Hudson. And, too, she was a part of that never-ending operation against the forces of evil—a reflection in which, as an honest woman, she must have found some satisfaction. Even some pride.

One does not minimize the genuine affection she came in time to have for Holmes and Watson, an affection shared, as she may have suspected, by some millions of the doctor's readers, any one of whom would have been happy to change places with her. And if her orderly soul was dismayed by cigars in the coal scuttle and tobacco in the toe-end of a Persian slipper, her protests in time, we may be certain, became mere humorous sallies which were responded to in kind. The sight of the detective's unanswered correspondence, transfixed by a jackknife in the center of his wooden mantelpiece, may have distressed her in the early days of his probation, but such vagaries—after a year or two—probably troubled her less than they troubled Watson, who had to live with them.

Her habits at the beginning of the relationship were probably more or less fixed. They changed, perhaps, or were adapted to her lodgers', as the years wore on. Apparently she went to bed about eleven, an hour after the maid. Waiting for Holmes to return from his pursuit of the mysterious old crone, in the course of the Lauriston Gardens investigation, Watson heard her "stately tread" as it passed the living room door. And presumably she rose early enough to satisfy Holmes and the doctor, who were not notoriously early risers. For all of them, it is clear, 7:15 was a bit unearthly on a cold spring morning. It was at that hour, early in April, 1883, that Watson blinked up at Holmes from his warm island of bedclothing and learned that Miss Helen Stoner had arrived from Stoke Moran, on the western border of Surrey.

Holmes obviously felt that an apology was in order. "Very sorry to knock you up, Watson," he said, "but it's the common lot this morning. Mrs. Hudson has been knocked up, she retorted upon me, and I on you."

But Mrs. Hudson had been affable enough; she had hurried down to light the fire and boil a pot of coffee. Watson, good fellow, was inclined to be a trifle curt until he had his coffee, a circumstance that possibly she remembered.

During the evening she was visited by her cronies. How numerous these were we cannot be certain, but they were numerous enough for a ring at the doorbell, on a stormy night, to suggest one such—rather than a client—to Sherlock Holmes. His conjecture that John Openshaw, whose ring had interrupted an evening of cross-indexing, was "likely to be some crony of the landlady's," was not, of course, borne out by fact; but it was a significant remark. No landlady is without her cronies, and we may be certain that the landlady of

Sherlock Holmes had cronies by the score. Her tales of her astonishing lodger and his companion must have made good telling for the shivering, envious women who sipped at tea or coffee with Mrs. Hudson (did they call her 'Udson?) of 221B Baker Street. Watson, himself, one ventures, told no more harrowing stories of prowess and of peril than Martha Hudson to her satellites.

Her staff, during the early days, was not a large one. There was a servant—alternatively called "the maid"—and just possibly a page in buttons; or it may be that the page was taken on a little later. His first recorded appearance, viewing the narratives in their chronological order, is in Watson's account of *The Yellow Face*, an episode dated in the month of April, 1882. It is possible that he was employed some months after the advent of the detective and the doctor, at a time when the increasing number of visitors calling upon Mr. Sherlock Holmes too frequently snatched the maid and Mrs. Hudson from their necessary household duties. Just conceivably he was a bit of swank on the part of Mrs. Hudson, who may well have looked forward to a time when she could afford a page, like other and more prosperous landladies. However that may be, he is not to be confused with a later page, called Billy, for whom Holmes entertained a considerable affection.

The establishment, then, was relatively small, and in all charity one cannot imagine Mrs. Hudson or her maid to have been overworked. There were no other lodgers we may be sure, at any time. Had there been others, Holmes would surely have complained of them (or they of him), and we should have some record of them in Watson's pages. Holmes and Watson themselves, of course, made work enough, but Mrs. Hudson's labors cannot at any time have been excessive. The famous living room, after all, was sacrosanct. From time to time, no doubt, the maid was allowed to enter—possibly under the watchful eye of Mrs. Hudson—for some imperative duty, but this would be only when the sternest necessity demanded it. Watson, in all likelihood, was agreeable enough to intrusion, but Holmes would not have cared to have domestics messing up his household gods. That the chamber was perennially untidy is one of the soundest of our certainties. One fancies Watson as making shift to keep the place in order, but there is a clear record of his despair. The principal duties of the maid upstairs, it may then be ventured, was making up the beds.

Throughout all of the Watsonian text there is the distinct suggestion that Mrs. Hudson did the cooking. Holmes bragged a little, in *The Sign of the Four*, about his "merits as a housekeeper"; but it was Mrs. Hudson, one feels certain, who cooked the oysters and the grouse. They were to be "ready in half an hour." Holmes merely ordered them from the shop—presumably while wearing a disguise described by Watson as suggesting "a respectable master mariner who had fallen into years and poverty." And it was quite certainly Mrs. Hudson who prepared the woodcock, during the excitements of the detective's search for the Blue Carbuncle. In view of the circumstances of that curious adventure, it will be remembered, Holmes thought of asking her to examine the bird's crop. This, to be sure, was after Watson had left his companion for a wife, but there is small reason to suppose that Mrs. Hudson gave over the task of cooking after the doctor's departure. Holmes dined at seven in those days, he told his friend when inviting him to return; although in point of fact it was considerably later before they actually got around to woodcock.

This admirable bird, incidentally, would appear to have been a favorite with Holmes. Among the ingredients of the "epicurean little cold supper," arranged by him for Lord St. Simon and the Moultons some years earlier, were a "couple of brace of cold woodcock, a pheasant, a *pâté-de-fois-gras* pie, with a group of ancient and cobwebby bottles." Mrs. Hudson had no hand in that proceeding, however; the dishes were from a caterer. They arrived during the detective's absence, greatly to the surprise of Watson. It is, of course, conceivable that Mrs. Hudson was away during the afternoon and evening of this event; but a more likely explanation is that Holmes—often a singularly thoughtful man —did not care to burden her with such an extensive and luxurious repast. It is also conceivable that he did not believe her quite up to such a spread. Sherlock Holmes had his own idea of Mrs. Hudson's abilities in a culinary way. In the final episode of *The Naval Treaty* she rose to an occasion and produced, in addition to ham and eggs, a dish of curried chicken for Percy Phelp's breakfast. "Her cuisine is a little limited," the detective testified on that occasion; "but she has as good an idea of breakfast as a Scotchwoman."

On the whole, it would appear that Mrs. Hudson was at her best where a breakfast was concerned; her staples were ham and eggs, with toast and coffee. These she prepared entirely to the liking of her lodgers, and, as we have seen, she was capable of rising to an occasion. When something more elaborate than curried chicken seemed to be in order, Holmes took the matter into his own hands and some provisioner was benefited. Nevertheless, she could prepare the traditional roast of beef, and did occasionally prepare it; it stood, when cold, upon the collaborators' sideboard until, presumably, they indicated that they were through with it. Fortunately for Holmes, there was a cold joint on hand during his investigation of the disappearance of the Beryl Coronet. It saved him from going hungry thoughout an arduous afternoon and evening.

But it is to be remembered that Holmes and Watson frequently dined out. In particular was this likely to be the case after some rather special triumph; and the strong probability is that Mrs. Hudson prepared no dinners without previous orders. When Holmes planned to dine at home, no doubt he told her of his intention. When he failed to leave instructions, he took potluck from the sideboard or hunted up a restaurant. "Dinner for two as soon as possible," was his order at the conclusion of the adventure of *The Mazarin Stone;* but it was probably something from the sideboard.

Tea was, from time to time, a pleasant possibility in the day's events, but for the most part the two men were well occupied from breakfast through to dinner, and even later. From the point of view of Mrs. Hudson the arrangement, all in all, may not have been the best imaginable, but, in the circumstances, it was the only arrangement possible.

Complicating even the simple routine of breakfast was the fact that Holmes rose fairly late, save when he was roused untimely, while Watson rose conspicuously later. Frequently as we see the friends together at the breakfast table—a pleasant tryst, and a favorite scene with most of the doctor's readers—it was actually not often that they entirely synchronized. Commonly Watson came down to find Holmes gone about his business, and at best it was his habit to enter the scene to the last rattle of his companion's coffee cup. Triumphant indeed must have been an occasion when Watson finished before Holmes; one such is recorded in the opening lines of *The Hound of the Baskervilles.* Sherlock Holmes, as we behold him, is still seated at the breakfast table, while Watson stands upon the hearthrug, examining the handsome stick left by Dr. James Mortimer the night before. Obviously he has already finished, and in the warm glow of comfortable satiety he dares to venture some pregnant observations of his own.

But the whole business of breakfast must often have been a little trying for Mrs. Hudson.

Years later the faintest possible clue emerges from Watson's text to suggest a change in the Baker Street domestic staff. In the opening scene of *Thor Bridge*, dated by inference in the early days of October, 1900, the unwelcome solidity of two hard-boiled eggs suggests to Sherlock Holmes a certain lack of interest on the part of a new cook. A *new cook*—the words are clearly printed in the record. But a new cook suggests an old cook, now vanished from the scene. And the original cook was certainly Mrs. Hudson. It is only a hint, but it might appear that somewhere along the years a cook was taken into the household and was in turn supplanted by another. If so, the probability is that the first one appeared at a time when Mrs. Hudson believed herself to be prosperous. Somewhere along in 1888, perhaps? By that time—we have Watson's word for it—Holmes's payments to his landlady had become quite "princely."

There is much for which we must always be grateful to Watson. He told what seemed to him important. But it never crossed his mind that we would ever care to know the exits and entrances of Baker Street domestics. Yet as more and more the interest of readers focuses on the life of Mr. Sherlock Holmes, every item of his association becomes enchanting. It is possible to deplore the doctor's reticence about the humbler lives that toiled obscurely in the echo of that sonorous reputation.

About the page, for instance. He had his uses. He held the door for those who had business with Mr. Sherlock Holmes and for those with whom Holmes had business. He held the door for clients entering and prisoners departing. It was an exciting enough existence for a lad. Two pages, at least, are indicated during the public career of the detective, and the last and best of them was Billy. His first appearance, unless Watson is confused, was at some time prior to the adventure called *The Valley of Fear*, in which episode, as recorded, he was already on the job. It was Billy, we are told, who showed Inspector MacDonald into the collaborators' living room. That was in January, 1887, and, as late as the summer of 1903—a long stretch—he was still apparently on the premises. In that year and season he greeted Watson, in the opening scenes of *The Mazarin Stone*, and made a significant remark. Watson, noting the dummy of the detective in the window, observed, according to the record: "We used something of the sort once before"—an obvious reference to the adventure of *The Empty House*, which occurred in April, 1894. And Billy replied that *that* had been before his time.

It is immediately evident that Watson *was* confused when he recorded the circumstance of MacDonald's arrival in 1887. In this matter we may safely trust to Billy, who would have a clearer memory of his employment than would the doctor. Unless, indeed, the earlier page was also called Billy; in which case it is difficult to see how the problem can be settled without greater confusion than already exists. In *The Noble Bachelor*, however, one of Holmes's cases that followed *The Valley of Fear* by only a few months, it was "our page-boy," in Watson's words, who threw open the door to announce Lord Robert St. Simon; there is no mention of any Billy. Nor was there in the earlier record of *The Yellow Face*, an odd mystery that came to Holmes in the spring of 1882. But it was clearly Billy who, on October 4, 1900, ushered Mr. Marlow Bates into the presence.

The actual change of pages took place, one fancies, some time after the adventure of *Shoscombe Old Place*, which occurred in the early summer of 1897; in Watson's account of that curious episode the page-boy is still nameless. The final proof would seem to lie in the doctor's record of 1903, at which time Billy was still "the young but very wise and tactful page, who had helped a little to fill up the gap of loneliness and isolation which surrounded the saturnine figure of the great detective." In spite of the "third person" form of narrative, the quoted words are too clearly Watson's own for any doubt to exist about their authorship. It is notorious that by

January, 1903, he had remarried, and the complacent utterance is precisely what he would have thought about the predicament of Holmes, after a few months of separation.

But in spite of the presence of a page upon the premises, it was Mrs. Hudson herself who sometimes announced the detective's visitors. There must have been some system about the matter, a private one that functioned consistently but without conscious thought perhaps, in her interesting mind. Class-consciousness, one thinks, had some bearing on the matter. Martha Hudson, a loyal and devoted servant of an indubitably higher type, was unquestionably a bit of a snob. Her exclamations of disgust, twice recorded, at the boisterous entrance of the ragged urchins led by Wiggins, are sufficient in themselves to urge the point; but it is her conduct in the instance of distinguished visitors that betrays her. These she ushered up the stairs herself and bowed them through the door. The case of Lady Hilda Trelawney Hope is typical; her card preceded her, majestically, upon the brass salver. And immediately before the Lady Hilda there had been the illustrious Lord Bellinger himself— "twice Premier of Britain." Such things were always happening. Watson would have been "guilty of an indiscretion" if he had even hinted at the identity of some of the illustrious clients who crossed the humble threshold in Baker Street, during one year, 1895. There is small question that Mrs. Hudson handled all such in person.

If the King of Bohemia appears to be an instance to the contrary—he climbed the steps in solitary splendor and rapped authoritatively on the door—it is to be remembered that, with all the richness of his attire, he was a rather terrifying figure, even for *fin de siècle* London, and it is probable that he snapped on his black vizard mask a little earlier than Watson thought. The doctor's deduction that he had adjusted it outside the living room door, because "his hand was still raised to it as he entered," is plausible and ingenious, but not necessarily the fact. He may simply have been testing it for security at that highly secret moment. To Mrs. Hudson he may well have seemed some wild bandit from the Balkans.

As summing up this amusing situation in the household, it may be suggested that where visitors or clients were of sufficient importance to warrant her attendance, Mrs. Hudson attended. For the rest, with exceptions, a humbler servant was quite good enough. Many, indeed, had no attendance at all after the outer door had been successfully negotiated; they climbed the seventeen steps alone, and knocked with their own knuckles. Where a visitor was familiar this was, of course, the rule. Hopkins, for instance, was allowed to go straight up, at any hour— as was the portly Mycroft, although he did not often call on his brother. In exceptional instances visitors were even allowed to enter the room in the absence of its tenants—a reckless business at best; but it is likely that by the case of Dr. Percy Trevelyan Mrs. Hudson's uncanny shrewdness in such decisions is attested. A "pale, taper-faced man with sandy whiskers," a haggard expression, and an unhealthy complexion, there can have been little enough about Trevelyan's outward appearance to recommend him. Holmes himself perhaps was hardly more apt at rapid diagnosis of a stranger than Mrs. Hudson on her outer threshold. What he caught by observation and deduction may have been little more, in substance, than that revealed to her by intuition. It is proverbial that landladies are that way.

As somewhat qualifying this view of Martha Hudson— this suggestion of a certain snobbishness, which in no wise detracted from her fundamental kindliness and amiability—it may be ventured that she was a woman of curiosity; that is, she was a woman. There can be no doubt that she was a witness to some strange, impulsive entrances and some remarkable exits. That her extraordinary lodgers fascinated her, from the beginning of the long association to its end, is certain. It follows that where curiosity struggled with decorum, she would frequently indulge her curiosity. One fancies that she appeared at times with visitors whose importance was less than their impatience, for no reason other than that their behavior roused her interest. Did she ever listen outside the door? The suspicion is uncharitable and unworthy— and probably entirely justified. Just for an instant perhaps—a moment—after the barrier had been closed, to catch the opening lines of the drama? Perhaps to verify her own conjecture that *this* was a saddening case of lovers parted? And this natural curiosity would mildly operate with reference to the living room. The very circumstance that her duties ended, for the most part, on the threshold, would make her more eager to cross over. The room itself was somewhat of a mystery, chaotically filled as it was with the detective's souvenirs of crime and comfort. For one reason and another, then, one thinks that Mrs. Hudson liked occasionally to get past the door, just to see what was going on. And while direct evidence is lacking, one thinks that she was not above a little innocent eavesdropping.

They were all busy enough, heaven knows—maid, page, and landlady—showing people up, or simply answering the doorbell. The doctor's narratives are filled with the tramp of feet upon the stairs. And it is certain that the bell rang many times in the course of a single morning and afternoon. When Watson, waiting in the rooms for his friend's return from an investigation, tells us that "every time a knock came to the door" he imagined it to be Holmes returning, he tells us also, by implication, that there were many knocks. Letters and cablegrams and newspapers were constantly arriving, particularly newspapers; one gathers that every new edition found its way into the consulting room. And coffee went up the stairs at almost mathematical intervals. No wonder there was a page boy and a maid, and even so it is probable that Mrs. Hudson kept her flesh down somewhat, with her constant climbing. "From the years 1894 to 1901 inclusive, Mr. Sherlock Holmes was a very busy man," reports the doctor, in the opening sentence of his account of *The Solitary Cyclist;* but almost equally busy, we may be sure, were Mrs. Hudson and her little staff of servants.

It is not surprising that she went to bed about eleven, and she was quite definitely between the blankets on that stormy night in late November, 1894, when the wheel of Hopkins' cab grated against the curb. It was Watson who had let the inspector in. "Run down, my dear fellow, and open the door," said Sherlock Holmes, on that occasion, "for all virtuous folk have been long in bed." That was the night they put Hopkins on the sofa, in preparation for an early start, next morning, for Yoxley Old Place. There was a train at six from Charing Cross to Chatham, and the humane Holmes did not rouse his slumbering landlady. They had coffee brewed on the detective's spirit lamp.

In Watson's sprightly narrative called *The Dying Detective* we have perhaps our clearest view of Mrs. Hudson, as she existed for the doctor. She was, he tells us, in his first sentence, "a long-suffering woman." "Not only," he continues, "was her first-floor flat invaded at all hours by throngs of singular and often undesirable characters, but her remarkable lodger showed an eccentricity and irregularity in his life which must have sorely tried her patience. His incredible untidiness, his addiction to music at strange hours, his occasional revolver practice within doors, his weird and often malodorous scientific experiments, and the atmosphere of violence and danger which hung around him made him the very worst tenant in London."

One can hardly question the characterization of either Holmes or Mrs. Hudson.

"On the other hand," proceeds the doctor, as if it ex-

89

plained everything, "his payments were princely. I have no doubt that the house might have been purchased at the price which Holmes paid for his rooms during the years that I was with him."

That is an assertion that opens up a subject with which we have no immediate concern—the matter of Holmes's profits. As it relates to the rental paid by the detective, it is possibly more extravagant than significant. The impecunious Watson was no judge of what was princely. It is clear, however, that Holmes paid his landlady a liberal sum, perhaps monthly, perhaps semimonthly, and it may be that Watson thought the amount excessive. It would be idle to deny that the circumstance had some relation to the detective's continued tenancy of the rooms and to Mrs. Hudson's regard for him. Certainly it is not the whole story, as Watson presently admits. "The landlady stood in the deepest awe of him," he tells us, "and never dared to interfere with him, however outrageous his proceedings might seem." *But* "she was fond of him, too," he confesses, "for he had a remarkable gentleness and courtesy in his dealings with women."

And a little later: "Knowing how genuine was her regard for him, I listened earnestly to her story when she came to my rooms in the second year of my married life and told me of the sad condition to which my poor friend was reduced."

Whatever may have been Mrs. Hudson's awe of Sherlock Holmes, and no doubt it continued throughout the years, her sincere affection for him cannot be questioned. She believed him to be dying when she rushed off to Watson on that November day in 1888. For three days she had seen him sinking, while he refused to allow her to call in a doctor, and her agitation was profound. Watson was horrified, and they drove back together to the rooms in Baker Street, Mrs. Hudson explaining all the way. "You know how masterful he is," she said. "I didn't dare to disobey him." Yet, "with your leave or without it, Mr.

Holmes," she had told him at last, "I am going for a doctor this very hour." It was not alone concern for a profitable lodger that dictated her decision. When Watson emerged from the sickroom, she was "waiting, trembling and weeping, in the passage." It is certain that she had been there throughout the entire scene within.

More than a year before, her affectionate concern for Holmes had been evident. During the excitements of the search for the Andaman Islander, she had been worried about the detective's health, and had even ventured—with a doctor in the house—to prescribe "a cooling medicine."

She would appear always to have been in excellent health herself. Possibly Watson looked after any small disorders that afflicted her while he was a partner in the firm, but a landlady with a cooling medicine in her cupboard would have her own ways of looking after her health. What she thought of Holmes's drug habits, until he abandoned them, is nowhere revealed, and the strong probability is that she never suspected them.

It is not strange that Holmes, in 1888, failed to take her into his confidence in the little comedy of *The Dying Detective;* in such dangerous matters he played a lone hand, and properly so. In smaller deceptions he made flattering use of her, as in the last scene of the adventure recorded as *The Naval Treaty,* when she conspired with him to serve up the missing papers under a breakfast cover. The innocent hoax tickled her immensely, one likes to think. To have a hand in any of her favorite lodger's enterprises must always have pleased her. Her sense of humor is not anywhere revealed as notable, however, and it is likely that it did not often rise above complicity in some such trickery as the episode of the naval papers. Doubtless there were a number of little pleasantries about the Persian slipper and the coal scuttle, and doubtless they became a bit familiar with repetition.

But the actual *adventures* of Mrs. Hudson were for a

number of years merely emotional states of heart and mind occasioned by the rumblings of the volcano on whose slopes she lived. They were lightning flashes on a horizon that was sometimes far off and sometimes close at hand. They were sounds and causes for apprehension from the living room room above; swift pictures of detective-inspectors arriving in haste and prisoners departing under duress; sinister figures on the doorstep. They were, in brief, the emanations from that atmosphere of violence and danger which made Mr. Sherlock Holmes, in Watson's considered phrase, "the very worst tenant in London." They were also, of course, the adventures in anticipation, as it were, of the innocent bystander, who, after all, is quite likely to be hurt in any disturbance of which he makes himself a part. Mrs. Hudson's adventures, in the more literal meaning of the word, possibly began with the determination of Professor Moriarty to discourage the attentions of Mr. Sherlock Holmes.

"No great harm was done" to the rooms in Baker Street, we are told, by the fire started there by Moriarty's agents, on a night in April, 1891, but the shock to Mrs. Hudson must have been considerable. We have no report of the actual damage done, other than Holmes's laconic comment. The newspapers of the following day carried an account of the outrage, from which it would appear that Holmes derived his own information. He was not in the rooms when they were set fire to, and Watson was at that time married and gone domestic ways. Unless she had a crony in, Mrs. Hudson was alone with her miniature staff of servants, and as such enterprises as arson are carried out at secret hours, the presumption is that they were all in bed. A pretty disturbance they must have had, and Mrs. Hudson undoubtedly sat up the rest of the night.

Thereafter came the tidings of Holmes's death in Switzerland.

"It was with a heavy heart that I take up my pen to write these last words in which I shall ever record the singular gifts by which my friend Mr. Sherlock Holmes was distinguished," wrote Watson, in beginning his account of *The Final Problem*. His heart, we may be sure, was no heavier than that of Martha Hudson. Only Mycroft, of the intimate circle, knew that Holmes survived, and what sentimental tale he told his brother's sorrowing housekeeper, to account for keeping up the rooms in Baker Street, we may only surmise. But it is quite possible that the admirable creature would have kept them up herself, merely for auld lang syne. One can imagine the tales with which she edified her cronies, during the three years of the detective's absence. And her melancholy perambulations of the famous living room, now at last wide open—like a museum—for her inspection.

But if she mourned for Holmes after the tidings of his death, the shock of his return produced an emotional disturbance even more intense; it threw her into violent hysterics. Small wonder, of course: Watson, himself, a little later, fainted for the first and last time in his life. Resurrection must always, one fancies, occasion dramatics more spectacular than the more familiar phenomenon of death. But she recovered from her shock when she realized that Holmes had need of her, and the adventure which followed was one of the high spots of Martha Hudson's life of service.

Holmes's plans had been quickly made. The remaining members of the gang, whose leader lay dead beneath the Reichenbach, knew that he had returned. Unknown to Mrs. Hudson, although probably suspected by brother Mycroft, they had watched the rooms with unceasing hatred, after the disappearance of Holmes, knowing that some day he would return. Incidentally, it is obvious that more of them escaped the police net than Scotland Yard admitted in its telegram to Holmes in Switzerland.

In the capture of the desperate Col. Sebastian Moran, Moriarty's underling, Mrs. Hudson played her part with intelligence and courage. Eight times in the course of two hours, while Holmes and Watson waited in the empty house across the way, the silhouetted shadow of the detective's bust changed its shape on the blind, as Martha Hudson, on her hands and knees, operated the facsimile in the lighted living room. Then the colonel's bullet shattered the window glass, passed accurately through the waxen skull, and flattened against the opposite wall. Mrs. Hudson picked it from the carpet as coolly as she would have lifted a penny.

Holmes was obliged to her for her assistance, and told her so—a trifle abruptly, it would appear from Watson's record of the scene; but it was sufficient for Mrs. Hudson. A laconic word of praise from Sherlock Holmes went a long way with those who served him. She was a bit distressed, however, by the ruin wrought by the Colonel's marksmanship. "I'm afraid it has spoiled your beautiful bust," she told the detective a little later, handing him the bullet.

The place had been put in order during Holmes's absence; his supposed death had furnished an opportunity for a straightening-up that Mrs. Hudson, for all her grief, had not failed to remark. "Our old chambers," wrote Watson, in *The Empty House*, "had been left unchanged, through the supervision of Mycroft Holmes and the immediate care of Mrs. Hudson. As I entered I saw, it is true, an unwonted tidiness, but the old landmarks were all in their places. There were the chemical corner and the acid-stained deal-top table. There upon a shelf was the row of formidable scrapbooks and books of reference which many of our fellow-citizens would have been so glad to burn. The diagrams, the violin-case, and the pipe-rack—even the Persian slipper which contained the tobacco—all met my eye as I glanced round me."

A happy homecoming, one must believe, for all of them. Thereafter, too, the relationship must have been somewhat closer. Holmes was never at any time demonstrative, even in his relations with Watson, and Mrs. Hudson was clearly a woman who knew her place and was careful to keep it. But it is impossible not to believe that a new warmth entered the situation after the detective's return from the dead. Holmes's proverbial distrust of the sex was surely qualified, after the adventure of *The Empty House*, by a distinguished exception made in favor of Mrs. Hudson. Later events, indeed, were to prove that he did hold both her courage and intelligence in the highest respect; so much so that in an hour of his own and his country's need, it was of Martha Hudson that he thought and to Martha Hudson that he turned for assistance.

Meanwhile, the old connections had been restored. In Baker Street, again, all was as it had been and must ever be. Watson, whose wife had died in the detective's absence, was back once more in his old room, and events were shaping toward the adventures of *The Second Stain* and *The Golden Pince-nez:* episodes dated in the last quarter of that memorable year 1894.

The years that followed were to bring to Holmes, and vicariously to Mrs. Hudson, some of the most surprising of his many experiences. Patrick Cairns, the murderer of "Black Peter" Carey, was to be captured in the rooms in Baker Street, after a struggle that, to Mrs. Hudson, must have been reminiscent of that which preceded the taking of Jefferson Hope. The wild-eyed and unhappy John Hector McFarlane was to clatter up the stairs with every evidence of madness; the portly Mycroft was to drive through yellow fog to his brother's doorstep, with tidings of sensational import; and Dr. Thorneycroft Huxtable, M.A., Ph.D., was to crash prostrate and insensible upon the bearskin rug. Illustrious clients in number were to cross the threshold of the consulting room, and Holmes was to refuse a knighthood for services that never have been revealed. Watson, good fellow, was to take another wife, though whose he took is still a matter much debated. Through all these scenes of triumph and disorder moved Martha Hudson on her daily round. Her figure, we may assume, grew thicker as the years went past, and possibly she climbed the stairs less often than had been her practice in earlier days. A hired cook, as we have seen, had for some years relieved her of the task of cooking. There was, one thinks, more leisure on her hands. It would be satisfying to know what use she made of it.

It has always been a minor mystery what relaxations she favored in her spare time, assuming that she had time to spare. There were her cronies, to be sure; but the cinema had not yet been developed. One fancies that she took to "patience," and later on—as we shall see—to knitting. When Holmes played upon his violin, we may be sure she sat and listened, rapt by the strains that also soothed and charmed the sentimental doctor. Madame Tussaud's was close at hand, and it is likely that its Chamber of Horrors displayed a murderer or two of Holmes's plucking. One sees her there on rainy afternoons, perhaps renewing old acquaintances.

What she thought of Watson's marriages is not included in the record. That she was fond of Mary Morstan can easily be imagined; and it may be that she wondered why the doctor, after his wife's death, did not at once return to Baker Street. She was not the sort, however, to venture comment on a delicate subject. Whomever Watson married, in 1902 or 1903, we may be certain that she offered her congratulations with good humor and sincerity. But Holmes's refusal of a knighthood must have tried her patience sorely.

In the matter of Sherlock Holmes's disguises, over the years of the relationship, it would be interesting to know what passed between them. There was a streak of mischief in the detective; it is impossible not to believe that he tried them out upon her, with amusing results. She had sharp eyes, and it may be assumed that if he passed their scrutiny unrecognized, he was content that others too would be deluded. It is notorious that he fooled Watson and Athelney Jones without half trying, but in Mrs. Hudson he must have recognized an intelligence of a different order. It is likely that sometimes she dismayed him. Like the landlady in Aristophanes, she may have asked, upon occasion: "Did you expect I would not know you again because yōu had buskins on?" Or words to that effect. With his more usual mummery she was, of course, familiar, and the spectacle of an asthmatic seafaring gentleman creeping up the stairs, believing himself unknown, just conceivably may have caused her to stand below and giggle.

Once in the early days Holmes called her Turner—Mrs. Turner. So Watson, at any rate, sets forth in *A Scandal in Bohemia*. "When Mrs. Turner has brought in the tray I will make it clear to you," said the detective, as alleged by Watson; meaning that he would make clear what service he demanded of the doctor. The remark has been anything but clear to students of the record. That Holmes actually made it may be doubted; it is too obviously the sort of error Watson would commit in the throes of composition. No doubt, at the moment of writing, a patient named Turner was waiting in his consulting room —was in some fashion, anyway, on his mind. The story was written by the doctor in 1891,[1] after the supposed death of Holmes in Switzerland, about an adventure dated in 1888; that is, it was written during the early weeks of his mourning for his friend, at a time when he was distraught. It is not for a moment to be supposed that Watson forgot the name of his old landlady, but it *is* a bit to his discredit, one thinks, that not once during the three years of Holmes's absence did he call upon her.

So they lived in Baker Street, and so always shall they live; the detective and the doctor and, below stairs, the humble and loyal housekeeper whose happiness it was to serve them. The actual term of the detective's tenancy

---

[1] It appeared in the *Strand Magazine* for July, 1891.

was from February, 1881,[2] until late in 1903—more probably until the early months of 1904. The date of Holmes's retirement from practice is not set forth by Watson; but in September, 1903, he was still actively engaged on the extraordinary adventure of *The Creeping Man*, and by December, 1904,[3] he had definitely retired to bee-keeping on the Sussex Downs. The hegira from London occurred some time in the months between, and the probabilities are perhaps in favor of a removal during the spring months of the latter year.

Thus ended the long Baker Street career of Mr. Sherlock Holmes, consulting specialist in crime, and with it, one thinks, Mrs. Hudson's tenancy of the premises made famous by her remarkable lodger. Whether she owned the building or rented it from another is not clear; but —although it is nowhere explicitly stated—there can be no reasonable doubt that she retired with Holmes to Sussex, if not at once, then later. Writing, in his retirement, of the curious mystery of *The Lion's Mane*, it is Holmes himself who furnishes the clue. "My house is lonely," he tells us. "I, my old housekeeper, and my bees have the estate all to ourselves." This was in 1926, in which year the detective published the reminiscence.[4] He was writing, however, of an adventure that occurred in 1907, and even then Mrs. Hudson was with him. It was she who first heard of the curious incident of Fitzroy McPherson's dog and mentioned it to Holmes, although he did not encourage gossip of the countryside.

Thereafter the record of her service is a blank until the second day of August, 1914, "the most terrible August in the history of the world." On that evening two

---

[2] *The Study in Scarlet* was called to his attention on March 4; during the "first week or so" there had been no callers.

[3] See *The Adventure of the Second Stain*, which was published in the *Strand Magazine* of December, 1904.

[4] In the *Strand Magazine* of December, 1926.

Sir Arthur Conan Doyle, the creator of Sherlock Holmes, in an oil painting (1897) by Sidney Paget and as he was photographed in 1923.

The first depiction of Sherlock Holmes at work, D. H. Friston's frontispiece to the first edition of *A Study In Scarlet*. The other figures (left to right) are Dr. Watson and inspectors Lestrade and Gregson of Scotland Yard.

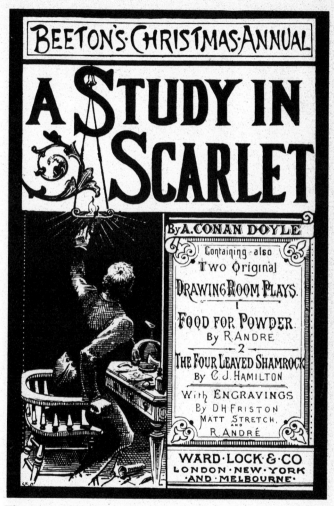

The cover of the now rare first edition of *Beeton's Christmas Annual* for 1887, which contained the first adventure of the great detective.

Baker St. The house described by Conan Doyle as the residence of Sherlock Holmes —. He is supposed to have occupied the second floor.

E.G.B.

221-B Baker Street, London, the residence of Sherlock Holmes, as discovered by Dr. Briggs. "The Empty House," known as Camden House, again courtesy of Dr. Briggs.

"The Empty House"
The arrow points to the words "Camden House." on the sign over the door.

G.C.B.

The Sherlock Holmes Inn, a popular London pub at 10 North-umberland St., near Charing Cross. It contains an extensive collection of Sherlockian "relics." Note the decorative paintings in the front windows.

Three theater playbills from the early 1900s, owned by Miss Kathleen Saintsbury and on display at the Sherlock Holmes Inn.

The famed Whitbread's Ale signboard at the Sherlock Holmes.

Dr. Watson and Sherlock Holmes discussing a case while riding in a railway coach, as illustrated by Sidney Paget, 1890. Could their chat be involved with the murder of John Straker?

Watson and Holmes, as portrayed by Nigel Bruce and Basil Rathbone, 1943, in one of the many American film versions of the great adventures.

Professor Moriarty, Holmes' relentless adversary and one of the greatest villains in all detective fiction. An illustration by Sidney Paget, 1893.

The "death" of Sherlock Holmes, as interpreted by Sidney Paget, 1893, for *The Memoirs of Sherlock Holmes*. Here we see Holmes and Moriarty locked in their deadly battle high in the Alps at Reichenbach Falls.

Basil Rathbone and Nigel Bruce keyholed as Holmes and Watson in the Hollywood production of *House of Fear*. Arthur Wontner as Holmes in a scene from the British film *The Triumph of Sherlock Holmes*.

From your friend
Sherlock Holmes
Basil Rathbone

William Gillette, who brought Holmes alive on the stage, in several of the many productions he starred in over the years.

Vincent Starrett, as a war correspondent in Mexico, 1914.

Watson and Holmes strolling along London's Regent Street...
and a bit suspicious of something in their view. By Sidney Paget,
to illustrate *The Hound of the Baskervilles.*

famous Germans stood upon the terrace of a house near Harwich. "Only one window showed a light behind them; in it there stood a lamp, and beside it, seated at a table, was a dear old ruddy-faced woman in a country cap. She was bending over her knitting and stopping occasionally to stroke a large black cat upon a stool beside her." With her self-absorption and "general air of comfortable somnolence," thought one of the Germans, she might have personified Britannia herself.

"Who is that?" asked Von Herling, the secretary of legation; and Von Bork replied: "That is Martha, the only servant I have left."

She looked with apprehension at the figure on the sofa, a little later, when Von Bork lay trussed and helpless, and seemed distressed that it was she who had brought him to that pass. "According to his lights," she said, he had been a kindly master. For two years she had served him faithfully, by Holmes's order, and at length she had betrayed him—the master spy of Germany. The dousing of her lamp had been the signal for the detective's entrance. It was Martha Hudson's last adventure, as far as it is possible for research to discover. In all things she had played her part to admiration, Holmes told the doctor: "I got her the situation when first I took the matter up." Once more in the history of the world, a woman's wit had saved a mighty nation from invasion.

She was to report to Holmes on the morrow at Claridge's Hotel, and there can be no question that they returned, in time, to their cottage on the Sussex Downs. It is a pleasant place in which, with Sherlock Holmes, she now passes her declining years, and they are eighty, each of them, if they are a day.[5] Mrs. Hudson, in all likelihood, is even older. Certainly she was no younger than Holmes

---

[5] Sherlock Holmes is believed to have been born in 1854; and this essay was written in 1934.

when he became her lodger. Her "stately tread," in 1881, would suggest at least a woman in her prime.

But it is proverbial that landladies never die.

"My villa," wrote Holmes in 1926, "is situated upon the southern slope of the Downs, commanding a great view of the Channel. At this point the coast-line is entirely of chalk cliffs, which can only be descended by a single, long, tortuous path which is steep and slippery. At the bottom of the path lie a hundred yards of pebbles and shingle, even when the tide is at full. Here and there, however, there are curves and hollows which make splendid swimming-pools filled afresh with each flow." It is a description richly filled with pictorial suggestion, and the possibilities turn one a little giddy. The wonder is that they do not break their necks.

In the evenings, if he still lives, Harold Stackhurst sometimes drops in for a chat and, probably, a cup of Mrs. Hudson's tea. We may imagine that the conversation runs a bit to bees and rheumatism, then swings to days and nights in Baker Street. Lucky Harold Stackhurst! Only occasionally does Watson visit them, which is perhaps unfortunate for the record. But Holmes, presumably, still adds a chapter, now and then, to that textbook which was to be the fruit of his declining years—which was to "focus the whole art of detection" into a single volume. The long winter evenings, when the bees and Mrs. Hudson have been sent to bed, should be an admirable time for literary composition.

7

THE

UNTOLD

TALES OF

DR. WATSON

"Somewhere in the vaults of the bank of Cox & Company, at Charing Cross," wrote Dr. Watson, in *Thor Bridge*, "there is a travel-worn and battered tin dispatch-box with my name . . . upon the lid. It is crammed with papers, nearly all of which are records of cases to illustrate the curious problems which Mr. Sherlock Holmes had at various times to examine."

Here is treasure trove, indeed!

For years the cry of a hungry populace has been for more tales of Sherlock Holmes—tales which Watson, who presumably still lives among us, has withheld for reasons of his own. We have listened to his explanations, at one time and another, and fatuously accepted them; but, really, do they explain? With Watson, we may deplore the circumstance that persons of high prominence continue to go on living, apparently to deprive us of revelations that are possible only after their demise; but surely the reputed modesty of Sherlock Holmes has functioned too often and too conveniently for the doctor.

The truth may be that Watson's ethical considerations mask a certain indolence and disinclination for which Holmes has been made to take the blame. There is little enough, in the long record of their association, to substantiate the doctor's assertions that Holmes was inflexibly opposed to publicity. At the moment of triumph, to be sure, he habitually waived his right to acclaim, in favor of his friends at Scotland Yard; but after the fact he was usually more than gracious to his biographer. Often he suggested the theme for one of Watson's contributions to the literature of crime; and at no time, save where the thing was morally impossible, can his objections have been more than a fitting depreciation of his own prowess.

On the other hand, the truth may be—in part, at any rate—that Holmes's acid humor was responsible for many of the tantalizing references to cases still unrecorded by his Boswell. His intentional mystification of his collaborator is frequently manifest in Watson's pages; what more likely than that the detective, in quizzical temper, whispered hints of extraordinary problems that actually had never come before him? That delicate service which he performed for the reigning family of Holland, perhaps? And the fascinating chapter suggested by the reference to Ricoletti of the Club Foot and his abominable wife.

Even so the battered tin dispatch box must contain problems of extraordinary interest—and how many little fingers would be sacrificed for just one more volume of them. What was the service for which Holmes refused a knighthood? What were the singular contents of the ancient British barrow? The Conk-Singleton forgery case was certainly in Watson's time and of his knowledge. It would be satisfying to know what anxiety agitated the Royal Family of Scandinavia.

There they lie, the materials for a hundred new stories, in the vaults of Cox & Company at Charing Cross.

But among the untold tales of Dr. Watson none has occasioned more scholarly perplexity than the "singular adventures of the Grice Patersons in the island of Uffa," one of several extraordinary cases that made the year 1887 memorable for Sherlock Holmes and his medical biographer. The reference is in *The Five Orange Pips,* fifth of the first group of tales, together with Watson's half-promise to return to it at some future date. But that was all we ever heard of the Grice Patersons or the island of Uffa. Even the island turned out to be *insula incognita,* a will-o'-the-wisp, an isle of illusion, unknown to geographers.

Thus matters stood for more than fifty years; but solution at last may be at hand. At least the mysterious island would appear to have been located. In one of the most brilliant identifications of our time, Dr. Jay Finley Christ of the University of Chicago discovered it single-handed, so to speak, although it had been under all our noses for years.

The parallels in the published writings of John H. Watson and James Boswell are well known. As early as the *Scandal in Bohemia* Holmes gave us the clue to the literary relationship between himself and Watson with the remark, "I am lost without my Boswell!" But there are dozens of instances that would be recognized without any clue whatever. Well, it was in Boswell's *Journal of a Tour to the Hebrides* that Uffa was found.

Boswell and Dr. Johnson made their visit to the Hebrides in 1773. Dr. Christ made his epochal discovery on or about June 18, 1945. Browsing happily in his Boswell, he came suddenly on the island of Ulva, and experienced a mild shock. To a Sherlockian the name suggested Uffa, but something further was needed for an identification. It was immediately forthcoming; in a few pages the startled professor was reading about the island of Staffa, and there they were—Ulva and Staffa—in literary proximity. Dr. Christ broke into a gentle perspiration, sat very still for a moment, then dashed for his globe, his maps, his gazeteer, and his encyclopedia. And there were Ulva and Staffa in geographical proximity too.

I pass over the ecstasy of that moment, although I envy Dr. Christ his luck. When he had somewhat recovered, he learned that Ulva and Staffa are two islands off the western coast of Scotland. They lie some six and one-half degrees west of Greenwich and about fifty-six and one-half degrees north of the equator. They are separated by some three miles of open water. Both were part of the estate of one Macquarrie and were sold under the hammer to pay his debts in 1777. Staffa is the smaller of the two, but as the scene of Fingal's Cave it would appear more likely than the other island to have been the scene of the Grice Patersons' singular adventure.

Bearing in mind Dr. Johnson's quarrel with the forger Macpherson, who wrote the epic poem *Fingal,* claiming to have translated it from the Gaelic of the ancient poet Ossian, it is perhaps possible to guess at the nature of the Grice Patersons' curious adventure. All the clues perhaps are in a book published a century before Watson met young Stamford in the Criterion bar and the magic syllables *Sherlock Holmes* were first heard in the world.

This tentative reading of the Grice Paterson riddle— the Patersons were almost certainly Scotch—depends to be sure upon Dr. Christ's identification of Uffa; in short, that Uffa never was Uffa at all, but a couple of other islands that Watson carelessly, or for reasons of his own, fused together in a plausible fiction. But can there be any doubt that Dr. Christ is right? If Ulva and Staffa were not the progenitors of Uffa, what were?

Hereafter, for the curious, is set forth in loose order

the presumptive titles of some of the many tales Watson did not tell. The muster is incomplete; it is a contribution only to the long list that fancy and deduction might contrive.[1]

The Case of Mrs. Cecil Forrester.

The Bishopsgate Jewel Case. (Inspector Athelney Jones will never forget how Holmes lectured the force upon it!)

The Trepoff Murder Case.

The Singular Tragedy of the Atkinson Brothers at Trincomalee.

The Dundas Separation Case.

The Adventure of the Paradol Chamber.

The Adventure of the Amateur Mendicant Society (whose members held a luxurious club in the lower vault of a furniture warehouse).

The Loss of the British Bark "Sophy Anderson."

The Singular Adventures of the Grice Patersons in the Island of Uffa.

The Camberwell Poisoning Case.

The Tankerville Club Scandal.

The Case of Mrs. Farintosh. (Which had to do with an opal tiara.)

Colonel Warburton's Madness.

The Little Problem of the Grosvenor Square Furniture Van.

The Tarleton Murders.

The Case of Vamberry, the Wine Merchant.

The Adventure of the Old Russian Woman.

The Singular affair of the Aluminium Crutch.

The Adventure of Ricoletti of the Club Foot and His Abominable Wife. (Most marvelous of all the missing titles.)

The Question of the Netherlands-Sumatra Company.

The Colossal Schemes of Baron Maupertuis.

The Manor House Case.

---

[1] The most complete list is to be found in H. W. Bell's *Sherlock Holmes and Dr. Watson.*

The Adventure of the Tired Captain. (Had Mr. E. C. Bentley this case in mind when he wrote *The Inoffensive Captain*?)

The Atrocious Conduct of Colonel Upwood. (In connection with the famous card scandal at the Nonpareil Club.)

The Case of Mme Montpensier.

The Papers of Ex-President Murillo.

The Shocking Affair of the Dutch Steamship "Friesland."

The Peculiar Persecution of John Vincent Harden.

The Sudden Death of Cardinal Tosca. (An investigation carried out at the personal request of His Holiness, the Pope.)

The Case of Wilson, the Notorious Canary Trainer.

The Dreadful Business of the Abernetty Family.

The Conk-Singleton Forgery Case.

The Repulsive Story of the Red Leech.

The Terrible Death of Crosby, the Banker.

The Addleton Tragedy. (And the singular contents of the ancient British Barrow.)

The Smith-Mortimer Succession Case.

The Adventure of the Boulevard Assassin.

The Case of Mr. Fairdale Hobbs.

The Dramatic Adventure of Dr. Moore Agar.

The Giant Rat of Sumatra. (A tale revealed in radio drama by Miss Edith Meiser, heaven bless her!)

The Case of Vanderbilt and the Yeggman.

The Hamerford Will Case.

The Case of Vigor, the Hammersmith Wonder.

The Arnsworth Castle Affair.

The Darlington Substitution Scandal.

The Case of Vittoria, the Circus Belle.

The St. Pancras Case.

The Delicate Affair of the Reigning Family of Holland.

The Case of Victor Lynch, the Forger.

The Incredible Mystery of Mr. James Phillimore (who, stepping back into his own house to get his umbrella, was never more seen in this world).

The Case of the Royal Family of Scandinavia.

The Case of the Royal Family of the Cutter "Alicia" (which sailed one spring morning into a small patch of mist from which it never again emerged).

The Intricate Matter in Marseilles.

The Affair of the Politician, the Lighthouse, and the Trained Cormorant.

The Strange Case of Isadora [sic] Persano (who was found stark staring mad with a matchbox in front of him which contained a remarkable worm said to be unknown to science).

Students should remember, also, that Watson frequently hinted at cases in which his friend was involved, without troubling to furnish clues. The important service for which Holmes refused a knighthood in 1902 is one of these, as is that matter of supreme importance arranged by the great detective for the government of France during the winter of the year 1890 and the early spring of 1891. And it is fairly certain that Shinwell Johnson figured as Holmes's underworld deputy in several cases other than that known to us as *The Illustrious Client*. During the early years of the century he was the detective's invaluable assistant in a number of curious matters.

8

"AVE

SHERLOCK

MORITURI

ET CETERA"

That is to say: Hail, Sherlock, we who shall one day pass and be forgotten, salute you, undying, who some say never lived!

Nevertheless, the day will come when Sherlock Holmes will be assumed to have left this world behind. It will be an assumption based on probability, since man may not live forever in the flesh.

When that word has been spoken there will be records and biographies in number, do not doubt, to prove the facts of his existence. In time, no doubt at all, he will have lived as surely in our world as ever he appeared to live in the years that marked his triumphs. There will be little placards on doors that once he entered and splendid memorials in the capitals of two hemispheres. Already, for the elect, there is that page of reminiscence by Opal, Lady Porstock; writing of her days in Parliament she reports:

I need only mention one other of my public activities, which remains a legitimate boast. It was a Private Member's Bill, brought forward by myself, that procured the erection of the great statue of Sherlock Holmes in Baker Street. I pointed out that London was now the only European capital which had no statue of the kind, and the plaque on No. 221B Baker Street was a quite inadequate recognition of the famous detective's services. The question whether he ever existed did not affect, or ought not affect, the feelings of veneration with which we regarded him. When the bill passed, I was elected a member of the Committee which was to decide between the various designs sent in. . . . I am glad to say that it was at my instigation the Committee chose the design sent in by Wrightman, then quite unknown, but destined to become famous as one of the leaders of the neo-classical school of the sixties. The conception is a noble one, and if some have found fault with the pipe as out of keeping with the classical draperies in which the figure is represented, it is not for us to complain.[1]

It may be a little early for admirers of Mr. Sherlock Holmes to look for the statue. Lady Porstock would appear to have been writing in the year 1988 of events that occurred between the years 1953 and 1959; and as her valuable reminiscences were edited by Ronald Knox in the year 1923, it is obvious that somebody is being spoofed. But one looks forward to Wrightman, and the coming of the great Baker Street memorial. Some years ago there was a railway engine wearing the famous name; it runs in and out of Baker Street Station, a sufficiently happy memorial of its kind.

As Lady Porstock has suggested, the question whether Sherlock ever existed has nothing to do with the case. His existence, however, is something more than an article

---

[1] R. A. Knox, *Memories of the Future.*

of mere faith. That he emerged from the pages of a book may be matter for scholarly inquiry; but it can scarcely be denied that he has taken his place in the living world. If you are in any doubt about it, just ask the first schoolboy you meet, or the first college president.

The famous General Humbert once embarrassingly asked for tidings of the detective. His dinner guest at the moment happened to be Sir Arthur Conan Doyle, then visiting the Argonne.

"A propos," snapped the general suddenly, his hard eyes fixed on the author's face, "Sherlock Holmes, est-ce qu'il est un soldat dans l'armée anglaise?"

There was an awkward moment, Then, "Mais, mon general," stammered the English novelist, "il est trop vieux pour service."

Is his mail still heavy, there on the Sussex Downs? Innumerable letters have been addressed to him at one time and another, and by some admirable citizens too. For the most part they were sent in care of Sir Arthur Conan Doyle; but even when they were not so directed the post office department of England—an intelligent institution —had no difficulty in making delivery.

A number of letters were received by Sir Arthur after his revelation that Holmes was retiring to a bee farm in Sussex. "Will Mr. Sherlock Holmes require a housekeeper for his country cottage at Xmas?" asked an "old fashioned, quiet woman," hopefully; and another spread her qualifications on the record: she was an adept, she said, at keeping bees and could "segregate the queen."

A professional lecturer who was also an apiarian specialist addressed himself to Sherlock Holmes direct, offering his services in a letter that is singularly charming in its spontaneity and gratitude:

Dear Sir:—I see by some of the morning papers that you are about to retire and take bee-keeping. I know not if this be correct or otherwise, but if correct

I shall be pleased to render you service by giving any advice you may require. I make this offer in return for the pleasure your writings gave me as a youngster; they enabled me to spend many and many a happy hour. Therefore I trust you will read this letter in the same spirit that it is written.

Autograph-hunters, too, were pestilential throughout the detective's long career, and doubtless are still troublesome. The more cunning of the tribe, hesitating to approach the celebrity directly, used to address their requests to Watson, urging his intercession. But the doctor's most upsetting communication must have been that dictated by a well-known press-cutting agency, suggesting that his brilliant confrere might care to take advantage of its service.

Most devout of all devout believers, perhaps, were those natives of Samoa whose incredible luck it was to have for master a certain Robert Louis Stevenson. Stevenson, relating his own inventions to his servants in the fragrant Pacific dusk, varied the evening program with some tales of Sherlock Holmes. In an amusing letter to his friend Conan Doyle, he complained of the difficulty of telling stories which every moment required a halt for explanations. What, asked the literal Samoans, was a railway? What was an engineer? Somehow, in spite of these handicaps, he put the tales across. "If you could have seen the bright feverish eyes of Simite," wrote the Scottish novelist, "you would have tasted glory."

O ye of little faith! Surely he lived; surely he breathed the fog and dust of Baker Street even as now he breathes the purer air that blows across the Sussex Downs.

But there is still considerable research to be done before those records for the future may be called complete —before the high history of Sherlock Holmes shall have been set down for posterity. When and where, precisely,

111

was he born? What was the college which for two years he attended? Who and what were his extraordinary parents? His brother Mycroft, that colossal genius, that all but fabulous monster, we have met casually on more than one occasion in the pages of Watson; but about the other members of the family circle Sherlock has been as close-lipped as a Scottish tradesman. Even to Watson he revealed so little of his early life that the doctor was at one time on the point of believing him an orphan, with no kinsfolk in the world. With the first mention of his brother Mycroft a few stray facts emerged.

"My ancestors," said Sherlock Holmes, on this unusual occasion, "were country squires, who appear to have led much the same life as is natural to their class. But, none the less, my turn that way [i.e., his ability to observe and make deductions] is in my veins, and may have come with my grandmother, who was the sister of Vernet, the French artist. Art in the blood is liable to take the strangest forms."

His grandmother—but on which side? The mother's, one supposes, since in general his ancestory were English country squires; and is there not perhaps a further clue to family history in Mycroft's name? Mycroft, the elder of two brothers (had there been others, Sherlock at this time should have mentioned them), might well receive his mother's family name—a common practice. Possibly Sherlock was their mother's surname, although indications point rather to a certain bowler of that name. Young Dr. Verner might resolve the tangle—if he still lives; and if he does, he is no longer young. He it was, it will be remembered, who purchased Watson's practice, in 1894, after the return of Holmes from Switzerland. He paid, it seemed to Watson, a ridiculously high price for so demure a practice; and it was not until some years afterward that Watson learned the truth—that Verner was, in fact, a distant relative of Holmes, and that it was Holmes who had provided the money. The connection here between the younger doctor and that grandmother who was sister to Vernet is obvious. Verner would be the English form of Vernet, or a corruption of the name after a year or so in England, and Dr. Verner would be a cousin of the detective twice or thrice removed.

However that may be, Holmes for two years, we know, attended college,[2] where the only friend he made was Victor Trevor—young Trevor whose father was a J.P. at Donnithorpe, in Norfolk. Old Trevor is, of course, quite dead; but it may be that Victor still survives, in which case there is another source of information. He was last heard of in the Terai, a successful tea-planter.

Again, in *The Musgrave Ritual*, there is just a whisper of Holmes's younger days. He speaks here, easily enough, of his "last years at the university"; but presumably it is just a figure of speech. The earlier record seems explicit, and it limits Holmes's formal college training to a scant two years. There is also mention of one Reginald Musgrave, with whom Holmes had some acquaintance at school. Apparently it was nothing intimate, for Musgrave was "not generally popular." Nevertheless, in Musgrave, if he survives—at Hurlstone Manor, in Western Sussex—there is another clue to Holmes's early exploits.

His first lodgings were apparently those in Montague Street (mentioned in *The Musgrave Ritual*), just around the corner from the British Museum. "There I waited," he told Watson, "filling in my too abundant leisure time by studying all those branches of science which might make me more efficient." And there it was his early clients came to him, among them Reginald Musgrave, whose puzzling problem was chronologically third on the list. Of the two earlier cases we have no word at all, unless we think of the Trevor business as one of them.

---

[2] Scholarly dispute still rages as to whether his university was Oxford or Cambridge.

Shortly thereafter it would appear that business picked up, and Sherlock Holmes looked round for larger quarters. He had been for some time, we must suppose, pursuing his curious studies in the chemical laboratory at St. Bartholomew's, where he had become known to young Stamford. All unwitting, and young as he still was, he was now at the turning point of his career. Almost around the corner—certainly no farther away than the Criterion bar—was Watson. And it was with Watson's wondering advent that the real career of Sherlock Holmes began.

Thereafter, the materials for a biography are numerous. It is of Holmes's younger days that we have need of further information. Is there no anecdote of the precocious youth's first startling piece of observation? His first recorded literary venture is a magazine article called "The Book of Life"; but it is certain that his famous monograph *Upon the Distinction between the Ashes of the Various Tobaccos* was already written—probably also some of his other less celebrated papers. Those long hours in the rooms in Montague Street would have been admirable for literary enterprise, and it seems likely that many of them were thus employed.

Some day, no doubt, there will be a *Collected Edition* of the famous writings. In the meantime, a bibliography may be useful, and this immediately follows.

The Writings of Mr. Sherlock Holmes

Upon the Distinction between the Ashes of the Various Tobaccos. "In it," says Holmes, "I enumerate one hundred and forty forms of cigar, cigarette, and pipe tobacco, with coloured plates illustrating the difference in the ash." *(Study in Scarlet, Sign of the Four, Boscombe Valley Mystery.)*

Upon the Tracing of Footsteps. "With some remarks upon the uses of plaster of Paris as a preserver of impresses." *(Sign of the Four.)*

114

Upon the Influence of a Trade upon the Form of the Hand. "With lithotypes of the hands of slaters, sailors, cork-cutters, compositors, weavers, and diamond-polishers." *(Sign of the Four.)*

The Book of Life. This was a magazine article on the science of deduction and analysis, based on the author's theories of systematic observation. It probably appeared some time early in 1881. *(Study in Scarlet.)*

On the Typewriter and Its Relation to Crime. As early as the late eighties Holmes contemplated the writing of this monograph, and there is no reason to suppose that it was not ultimately written. *(Case of Identity.)*

Upon the Dating of Old Documents. "The *terminus a quo* of this monograph is uncertain," says S. C. Roberts. "It probably dealt in the main with the problem of handwriting from the sixteenth century onwards. It was completed before the year 1889, and at a later date Holmes was engaged in the study of the mediaeval aspect of the subject." *(Hound of the Baskervilles* and *Golden Pince-nez.)*

Of Tattoo Marks. "I have made a small study of tattoo marks," says Holmes, "and have even contributed to the literature of the subject." His paper included an examination of the curious pink pigment used by Chinese artists. *(Red-Headed League.)*

On Secret Writings. "I am fairly familiar with all forms of secret writings," Holmes asserts, "and am myself the author of a trifling monograph upon the subject, in which I analyze one hundred and sixty separate ciphers." *(Dancing Men.)*

On the Surface Anatomy of the Human Ear. There were two short monographs on this subject, in the *Anthropological Journal,* apparently some time in the early eighties. Both papers appeared during the one year, and one may well have been an amplification of the other. *(Cardboard Box.)*

Early English Charters. It is not certain that this work ever was completed. Holmes conducted laborious researches in the subject, however, in the year 1895, which led to such striking results that Watson half promised to make them the subject of one of his own narratives—a promise which has not as yet been fulfilled. *(Three Students.)*

On the Polyphonic Motets of Lassus. Printed for private circulation, possibly some time in 1896, certainly after 1895. The work is said by experts to be the last word on the subject. *(Bruce-Partington Plans.)*

Chaldean Roots in the Ancient Cornish Language. Holmes began his study of this subject in the spring of 1897 if Watson is correct, and although the adventure of *The Devil's Foot* occurred to interrupt him, it is certain that he returned to it. *(Devil's Foot.)*

Malingering. A monograph upon a subject which interested Holmes at the time of the adventure of *The Dying Detective.* While it is not certain that it ever was written, it may very well have been. *(Dying Detective.)*

Upon the Uses of Dogs in the Work of the Detective. It was in 1903 that Holmes first mentioned his intention to write this monograph, but there is no report in Watson on its publication. *(Creeping Man.)*

Practical Handbook of Bee Culture, with Some Observations upon the Segregation of the Queen. This magnum opus of the detective's later years was written after his retirement, and was published some time prior to August, 1912. Presumably it is a small 12mo. It was issued in blue cloth, lettered in gold. *(His Last Bow.)*

The Blanched Soldier. The first of the detective's criminal reminiscences to be set forth by himself. The adventure occurred in January, 1903, but this account of it was written many years later. It was first published in the *Strand* during 1926. Available in all editions of *The Case-Book of Sherlock Holmes. (Blanched Soldier.)*

The Lion's Mane. Second and last of Holmes's adventures related by himself. The episode is dated in July of 1907, but the reminiscence was probably penned at about the same time as *The Blanched Soldier.* Published in the *Strand* during 1926. Available in all editions of *The Case-Book of Sherlock Holmes. (Lion's Mane.)*

Sigerson. It was during the year 1893 that the English

116

newspapers carried accounts of the "remarkable explorations of a Norwegian named Sigerson," who had traveled for two years in Tibet and spent some days with the head Lama, at Lhassa. Sigerson is now known to have been Holmes himself, then believed to be dead; and while the newspaper reports are no doubt interviews rather than firsthand accounts, they will be of the highest interest to all Holmes collectors, and are mentioned here to complete the record. *(Empty House.)*

The Whole Art of Detection. Sherlock Holmes proposed to devote his declining years to the composition of this textbook, which was to "focus the whole art of detection into one volume." He mentioned it to Watson on a cold morning in the winter of 1897, and there is no reason to suppose that he ever gave over the fascinating idea. As the volume has not yet been announced, it may be assumed that it is still in preparation. *(Abbey Grange.)*

Translations. The number of Holmes's works that have been translated into foreign languages is probably large, and no attempt has been made to run them all to earth. Certain it is that as early as 1888 François le Villard was engaged in translating into French the writings then published. The two criminal reminiscences (see above) have appeared in practically *all* languages, including the Scandinavian.

Look well, then, for these rare and difficult titles, Bookmen, for your own shelves and for the records of the future. They will come hard and perhaps high; but they will be worth the effort.

9

THE

REAL

SHERLOCK

HOLMES

But one must drop at last the happy pretense and admit that Sherlock Holmes is dead. And being dead yet liveth. The paradox is complete; the tale is ended. The most famous fathomer of the modern world has gone upon his final quest, the most mysterious of all his strange adventures.

He died July 7, 1930, at his home in Crowborough, Sussex—he called it Windlesham—in the person of the man who had created him. For true as it may be that the model for the immortal detective was Dr. Joseph Bell of Edinburgh, there is no doubt that the real Holmes was Conan Doyle himself. In innumerable ways throughout his life of extraordinary service the British novelist proved the truth of that controversial matter. From first to last—as student, physician, writer, spiritualist, and prophet of the war—he was always the private detective, the seeker after hidden truths, the fathomer of obscure mysteries, the hound of justice on the trail of injustice and official apathy.

It was inevitable that the author of the Sherlock Holmes stories should often be called upon to enact the role of his imaginary detective, and sometimes he accepted the implied challenge. Twice in his career he undertook fatiguing causes because he believed that justice had not been done. The cases of George Edalji and Oscar Slater were notorious in their day. They shook all England, and the thunder of Conan Doyle's denunciations crossed the Atlantic.

There is a flavor of Holmes in both episodes—that pinch of the bizarre, bordering on the fantastic, that marks most of the fictional adventures. Chronologically the Edalji case stands first. The facts are as follows:

George Edalji, a young law student, was the son of the Rev. S. Edalji, a Parsee, vicar of the Anglican parish of Great Wyrley, whose wife was an Englishwoman. The vicar was a kindly and intelligent man who performed his churchly duties with fidelity; his spouse was an excellent wife. Their son, the half-caste George Edalji, was a young man of irreproachable character, an admirable student who had won the highest honors in his legal studies. However, the situation was unfortunate. "How the vicar came to be a Parsee," wrote Conan Doyle, "or how the Parsee came to be the vicar, I have no idea. Perhaps some Catholic-minded patron wished to demonstrate the universality of the Anglican church. The experiment will not, I hope, be repeated, for though the vicar was an amiable and devoted man, the appearance of a coloured clergyman with a half-caste son in a rude, unrefined parish was bound to cause some regrettable situation." [1]

The family became the target of considerable local malice and was for a time subjected to a veritable

---

[1] A. C. Doyle, *Memories and Adventures*.

broadside of anonymous letters, many of them "of the most monstrous description." Shortly thereafter an epidemic of horse-maiming broke out, and these outrages lasted for a considerable period. The police accomplished next to nothing until popular clamor forced an activity; then a hurried investigation was made and George Edalji was arrested for the crime—that is, for the crime of horse-maiming. The principal evidence against him was found in certain of the anonymous letters, in which the writer hinted at a knowledge of crimes involving horses. It was asserted that George Edalji had written the letters which for so long had plagued his family.

This evidence, as later pointed out by Conan Doyle, was incredibly weak; yet the police, "all pulling together and twisting all things to their end," secured a conviction and the prisoner was sentenced to seven years' penal servitude. This was in 1903.

It was not until late in 1906 that Sir Arthur heard of this somewhat obscure case; then a statement of it in an unimportant journal caught his eye. "As I read," he wrote later, "the unmistakable accent of truth forced itself upon my attention and I realized that I was in the presence of an appalling tragedy, and that I was called upon to do what I could to set it right." This included a careful reading of everything he could obtain bearing on the case, a study of the trial record, a visit to the family of the condemned man, and a tour of investigation over the scene of the several crimes.[2] Early in 1907 he began publication of a series of articles analyzing the evidence, and shortly England and the English-speaking world was ringing with the wrongs of George Edalji.

In his autobiography Sir Arthur wrote:

If the whole land had been raked, I do not think it

---

[2] A. C. Doyle, *The Case of Mr. George Edalji.*

would have been possible to find a man who was so unlikely, and indeed so incapable of committing such actions. Nothing in his life had ever been urged against him. His old schoolmaster with years of experience testified to his mild and tractable disposition. He had served his time with a Birmingham solicitor, who gave him the highest references. He had never shown traits of cruelty. He was . . . devoted to his work . . . and he had already at the age of twenty-seven written a book upon Railway Law. Finally, he was a total abstainer, and so blind that he was unable to recognize anyone at the distance of six yards. It was clear that the inherent improbability of such a man committing a long succession of bloody and brutal crimes was so great that it could only be met by the suggestion of insanity. There had never, however, been any indication even of eccentricity in George Edalji. On the contrary, his statements of defense were measured and rational, and he had come through a series of experiences which might well have unhinged a weaker intellect.

One hears the familiar voice of Sherlock Holmes himself in such a statement.

It had been charged at the trial that Edalji had committed the mutilations for which he was being tried at some time in the evening. The prisoner was able to prove an unshakable alibi, however, so the police dexterously shifted ground and advanced a new theory—to wit, that the crimes had been committed in the early hours of the morning. As against this, it was shown that George Edalji slept in the same room as his father, the Parsee vicar, who was not only a light sleeper but had the habit of locking the door of the chamber each night before he retired. The vicar swore that his son had not left the room during the night.

"This may not constitute an absolute alibi in the eye of the law," comments Sir Arthur dryly, "but it is difficult to imagine anything nearer to one unless a sentinel had been placed outside the door all night."

121

But the defense of Edalji was weakly conducted. As far as Conan Doyle was able to discover, no mention ever was made of the fact that the prisoner was virtually blind—except in a good light—while between his home and the scene of the mutilations stretched the breadth of the London and North-Western Railway, a complex expanse of rails and wires and other obstacles, with hedges on either side, difficult enough for any man to pass in daylight.

All of which, and much more, was set forth by Sir Arthur in his indignant article; and so great was the storm he stirred up that a government committee was appointed to examine and report. The finding, when at length it came to hand, was a compromise. The committee was severe enough about the condemnation of Edalji and could find no evidence to associate him with the crime, but it clung stubbornly to the old theory that he had written the anonymous letters (which were in two handwritings) and had been, therefore, himself contributory to the miscarriage of justice. Edalji was freed but was denied compensation for his long incarceration.

"A blot upon the record of English justice," Sir Arthur called it in his comment on the report, and added: "It is to be remembered that the man was never tried for writing the letters—a charge which could not have been sustained—so that as the matter stands he has got no redress for three years of false imprisonment, on the score that he did something else for which he has never been tried."

But Sir Arthur in his Sherlockian explorations at Wyrley had found what seemed to him a direct clue to the writer or writers of the letters, and also to the identity of the mutilator or mutilators. In *Memories and Adventures* he tells us:

I became interested, the more so as the facts were

very complex and I had to do with several people who were insane as well as criminal. I have several letters threatening my life in the same writing as those which assailed the Edaljis—a fact which did not appear to shake in the least the Home Office conviction that George Edalji had written them all. . . . The mistake I made was that having got on the track of the miscreant, I let the police and the Home Office know my results before they were absolutely completed. There was a strong prima facie case, but it needed the good will and the cooperation of the authorities to ram it home. That cooperation was wanting. . . . The law officers of the Crown upheld their view that there was not a prima facie case. . . . Let me briefly state the case that the public may judge. I will call the suspect "X." I was able to show:

1. That "X" had shown a peculiar knife or horse-lancet to someone and had stated that this knife did the crimes. I had this knife in my possession.

2. That this knife or a similar knife must have been used in *some* of the crimes, as shown by the shallow incision.

3. That "X" had been trained in the slaughter-yard and the cattleship, and was accustomed to brutal treatment of animals.

4. That he had a clear record both of anonymous letters and of destructive propensities.

5. That his writing and that of his brother exactly fitted into the two writings of the anonymous letters. In this I had strong independent evidence.

6. That he had shown signs of periodical insanity, and that his household and bedroom were such that he could leave unseen at any hour of the night.

There were very many corroborative evidences, but those were the main ones, coupled with the fact that when "X" was away for some years the letters and outrages stopped, but began again when he returned. On the other hand, when Edalji was put in prison the outrages went on the same as before.

A very workmanlike summary, and worthy of Sherlock Holmes at his best. It may be added that Sir Arthur later learned that the individual referred to as "X" had been convicted a number of times and for a number of crimes including arson, theft, and damage. Nothing ever was done for Edalji, however, after his release—except by individuals. "He came to my wedding reception," Conan Doyle has recorded, "and there was no guest whom I was prouder to see."

The Slater case, the celebrity of which was greater than that of George Edalji, came to the novelist-detective as a result of the earlier investigation. It was assumed by Slater sympathizers that what Sir Arthur could do for one man he could do for another. "I went into the matter most reluctantly," he confesses in his autobiography, "but when I glanced at the facts, I saw that it was an even worse case than the Edalji one, and that this unhappy man had in all probability no more to do with the murder for which he had been condemned than I had. I am convinced that when on being convicted he cried out to the judge that he never knew that such a woman as the murdered woman existed he was speaking the literal truth."

The victim was a Miss Marion Gilchrist, an elderly spinster living in Glasgow. She was murdered in her flat, in which she had lived for thirty years, on December 21, 1908. Her servant, Helen Lambie, was away at the time —purchasing a newspaper—and it was during her ten-minute absence that the murder was committed. Returning from her errand, the servant found a young man named Adams at the Gilchrist door, ringing the bell. He was from the flat below. He and his sisters had heard a noise above (in Miss Gilchrist's apartment) and a heavy fall, and he had been sent upstairs to ascertain what had happened. The servant opened the door with her key. Then as they hesitated on the threshold, a man appeared from within, who approached them pleasantly, seemed about to speak, but instead passed them and rushed down the stairs. In the dining room the body of Miss Gilchrist was found, the head brutally beaten in and covered with a rug.

In spite of the fact that Miss Gilchrist was the possessor of a valuable collection of jewelry, robbery would appear not to have been the motive for the murder, since all that was missing was a crescent diamond brooch worth possibly £50. A box of papers had been broken open and the contents scattered. The description of the man as reported by Adams and Helen Lambie was not particularly good—they were in some disagreement—and it was not at all the description of Oscar Slater, a German Jew by extraction, who was ultimately arrested and condemned for the crime.

The apprehension of Slater came about because he had pawned a diamond brooch just before starting for America. New York was warned of his prospective advent on American shores and he was arrested and returned to Glasgow, where it was discovered beyond a question of doubt that the brooch in question had been in his possession for years and never had belonged to Miss Gilchrist.

The public had lost its head, however, and the police were in similar state. Slater was poor and without friends. His morals were shown not to have been of the highest, and Scottish virtue was shocked. A card of tools was found in his belongings; it was alleged that the hammer of the set had been the instrument of death. The description of the man seen by Adams and Helen Lambie was amended to fit Slater. The two principal witnesses were not sure, but thought the man they had seen in the hallway *might* have been the prisoner. Slater was in bad case. He proved a clear alibi, but as his witnesses were his mistress and his servant girl it was not allowed. No attempt ever was made to show a connection between

Slater and Miss Gilchrist, or between Slater and anybody in the house occupied by Miss Gilchrist. He was a stranger in Glasgow. At the trial he was not very well defended, and the Crown ultimately won a conviction—under Scottish law—by a vote of nine ballots to six. Slater was condemned to death, the scaffold was erected, and two days before the day set for the execution the sentence was commuted. He was resentenced to life imprisonment and was serving his sentence when Conan Doyle became interested in his plight.

In Sir Arthur's brilliant pamphlet, *The Case of Oscar Slater*, now a rarity, there is all the fascination of a tale from the chronicles of Sherlock Holmes. Many of its assertions, dogmatic and otherwise, might indeed have been quoted directly from those old pages. Is not this, for instance, the veritable accent of Holmes, talking to the faithful Watson?

> The trouble, however, with all police prosecutions is that, having once got what they imagine to be their man, they are not very open to any line of investigation which might lead to other conclusions. Everything which will not fit into the official theory is liable to be excluded. One might make a few isolated comments on the case which may at least give rise to some interesting trains of thought.

And, for a beginning, Sir Arthur wonders if the murderer was really after the jewels at all. . . .

> When he reached the bedroom and lit the gas, he did not at once seize the watch and rings which were lying openly exposed upon the dressing-table. He did not pick up a half-sovereign which was lying on the dining-room table. His attention was given to a wooden box, the lid of which he wrenched open. The papers in it were strewed on the ground. Were the papers his object,

126

and the final abstraction of one diamond brooch a mere blind?

But, supposing the murderer to have been indeed after the jewels,

it is very instructive to note his knowledge of their location, and also its limitations. Why did he go straight into the spare bedroom where the jewels were actually kept? The same question may be asked with equal force if we consider that he was after the papers. Why the spare bedroom? Any knowledge gathered from outside (by a watcher in the back-yard, for example) would go to the length of ascertaining which was the old lady's room. One would expect a robber who had gained his information thus, to go straight to that chamber. But this man did not do so. He went straight to the unlikely room in which both jewels and papers actually were. Is not this remarkably suggestive? Does it not pre-suppose a previous acquaintance with the inside of the flat and the ways of its owner?

But now note the limitations of the knowledge. If it were the jewels he was after, he knew what room they were in, but not in what part of the room. A fuller knowledge would have told him they were kept in the wardrobe. And yet he searched a box. . . . To this we may add that he would seem to have shown ignorance of the habits of the inmates, or he would surely have chosen Lambie's afternoon or evening out for his attempt, and not have done it at a time when the girl was bound to be back within a very few minutes. What men had ever visited the house? The number must have been very limited. What friends? what tradesmen? what plumbers?

Surely that is all good Sherlock Holmes, as—even more brilliantly—is this:

How did the murderer get in if Lambie is correct in thinking that she shut the doors? I cannot get away from the conclusion that he had duplicate keys. In that case all becomes comprehensible, for the old lady—whose faculties were quite normal—would hear the lock go and would not be alarmed, thinking that Lambie had returned before her time. Thus, she would only know her danger when the murderer rushed into the room, and would hardly have time to rise, receive the first blow, and fall, as she was found, beside the chair upon which she had been sitting. But if he had *not* the keys, consider the difficulties. If the old lady had opened the flat door her body would have been found in the passage. Therefore, the police were driven to the hypothesis that the old lady heard the ring, opened the lower stair door from above (as can be done in all Scotch flats), opened the flat door, never looked over the lighted stair to see who was coming up, but returned to her chair and her magazine, leaving the door open and a free entrance to the murderer. This is possible, but is it not in the highest degree improbable? Miss Gilchrist was nervous of robbery and would not neglect obvious precautions. The ring came immediately after the maid's departure. She could hardly have thought that it was her [*sic*] returning, the less so as the girl had the keys and would not need to ring.

The only alternatives to this reasoning, ventured Sir Arthur, were that "the murderer was actually concealed in the flat when Lambie came out, and of that there is no evidence whatever, or that the visitor was someone whom the old lady knew, in which case he would naturally have been admitted."

The narrative points out that, although the crime was a singularly bloody one, no marks of blood were found on match or matchbox, and none upon the wooden box opened in the bedroom. "It has never been explained why a rug was laid over the murdered woman. . . . It is at least possible that he [i.e., the murderer] used the rug as a shield between himself and his victim while he bat-

128

tered her with his weapon. His clothes, if not his hands, would in this way be preserved."

In a brilliant examination of the evidence produced at the trial, the novelist questions the qualities of the witnesses, stresses the important fact that a knowledge of Miss Gilchrist's jewel collection was not, at the time of the murder, confined to the inmates of the house, and emphasizes the significant circumstance that a dog belonging to Miss Gilchrist had been poisoned in September of the year 1908—that is to say, more than a month before Slater arrived in Glasgow and more than two months before the murder. In his pamphlet he is very severe upon the Scottish Lord-Advocate who conducted the prosecution.

All in all, it is a masterly document, ringing in every line with the curt inflections of Sherlock Holmes himself, and charged with that detective's hard logic and common sense. However, it was to no immediate avail. The novelist's newspaper campaign stirred England and even brought about another government commission to inquire into the affair; but nothing came of it, and Slater was allowed to languish in prison.

A strange aftermath of the case is recorded by Sir Arthur in his autobiography. Shortly after the trial of Slater, messages were received in a spiritualist circle, which purported to come from the murdered woman. She was asked what weapon had slain her, and replied that it had been an iron box-opener—a singularly satisfying answer, according to Conan Doyle, considering the peculiar nature of the wounds upon the head. The writer also asserts that the name of the murderer was asked and a reply given, but he does not reveal what it was.

There for years the unhappy affair rested. From time to time, as Slater's incarceration lengthened, efforts were made to reopen the case, but not until nineteen years after the conviction were Sir Arthur's activities successful. Then, at long last, Slater was released—in July, 1928. According to newspaper reports, he accepted a government offer of £6,000 as compensation for his wrongs; then with strange ingratitude refused to repay a sum of money guaranteed by Doyle before the retrial at which he was acquitted.

Minor mysteries were frequently presented for Sir Arthur's solution, and it was his pleasure, when in a detectival mood, to put his wits to work on them. In one, the habits of thought made familiar by Mr. Sherlock Holmes of Baker Street were copied with entire success. The case was that of a man who had disappeared after withdrawing his bank balance of £40, for which sum it was feared he had been slain. The last trace of the supposed victim was at a hotel in London; he had come up from the country only that morning. In the evening he was known to have visited a theater, then to have returned to his hotel and changed from his evening garments into walking clothes. This evening raiment was found the next day in his room. No one saw him leave the hotel, but a guest in a neighboring room stated that he had heard the man moving about during the night. A week had elapsed when the novelist was consulted, and the police had discovered exactly nothing. A perfect opening for an adventure of Sherlock Holmes.

The facts were communicated by relatives of the missing man living in the country, and Sir Arthur answered by return post that, obviously, the vanished citizen was either in Glasgow or Edinburgh. It was later proved that he had gone to Edinburgh. One can almost hear the cry of the admiring Watson, "Wonderful, my dear Holmes!" —and the retort of the detective, "Elementary, my dear Watson, elementary!"

In *Memories and Adventures* Sir Arthur explains:

The one advantage which I possessed was that I was

familiar with the routine of London hotels. The first to look at the facts and separate what was certain from what was conjecture. It was *all* certain except the statement of the person who heard the missing man in the night. How could he tell such a sound from any other sound in a large hotel? That point could be disregarded if it traversed the general conclusions. The first deduction was that the man had meant to disappear. Why else should he draw all his money? He had got out of the hotel during the night. But there is a night porter in all hotels, and it is impossible to get out without his knowledge when the door is once shut. The door is shut after the theatre-goers return—say at twelve o'clock. He had come from the music-hall at ten, had changed his clothes, and had departed with his bag. No one had seen him do so. The inference is that he had done it at the moment when the hall was full of the returning guests, which is from eleven to eleven-thirty. After that hour, even if the doors were still open, there are few people coming and going, so that he with his bag would certainly have been seen.

Having got so far upon firm ground, we now ask ourselves why a man who desires to hide himself should go out at such an hour. If he intended to conceal himself in London he need never have gone to the hotel at all. Clearly then he was going to catch a train which would carry him away. But a man who is deposited by a train in any provincial station during the night is likely to be noticed, and he might be sure that when the alarm was raised and his description given some guard or porter would remember him. Therefore, his destination would be some large town which he would reach as a terminus where all his fellow passengers would disembark and where he would lose himself in the crowd. When one turns up the time-table and sees that the great Scotch expresses bound for Edinburgh and Glasgow start about midnight, the goal is reached. As for his dress suit, the fact that he abandoned it proved that he intended to adopt a line of life where there were no social amenities. This deduction also proved to be correct.

In another case, involving a young woman engaged to be married to a foreigner, the man also disappeared, and by a similar process of reasoning Sir Arthur was able to show where he had gone and how unworthy he was of his fiancée's affection.

Not all the novelist's detectives cases, however, were as successful as these. He relates with great gusto how, on the occasion of a burglary within a stone's throw of his own home, the village constable—with no theories at all —had actually seized the culprit when he (Sir Arthur) had got no farther than the Sherlockian conclusion that the man was left-handed and had nails in his shoes.

Even in his spiritualistic investigations, which occupied the later years of his life to the exclusion of almost everything else, the novelist was at all times the detective, applying the methods of his most famous fictive character to the obscure problems of psychic phenomena. A few years before his death he examined the curious claim of a number of children that they had seen and photographed living fairies; he even published a volume on the subject. To the end he was a remarkable example of the scientific investigator touched with the curiosity and credulity of a child—an admirable blend, it would seem, for the perfect sleuth.

10

PORTRAYERS

OF

SHERLOCK

HOLMES

There is a line of text in Watson from which we learn that all emotions, but particularly that of love, were abhorrent to the "cold, precise but admirably balanced mind" of Mr. Sherlock Holmes. Nevertheless it is of record that Holmes once fell in love and married. Since it was only on the stage, perhaps it does not count. Miss Alice Faulkner was the woman in the case, and as recently as 1930 her golden head was lying on the detective's shoulder at curtain fall.

The year was 1899 when this surprising situation was first publicly acknowledged; it shared attention with the Boer War. Arthur Conan Doyle, still three years away from knighthood, received a sudden wire from an American actor who had obtained permission to write a play called *Sherlock Holmes*.

"May I marry Holmes?" the cable asked; and Conan Doyle, then worrying about the war and how he might get into it, replied: "You may marry or murder or do what you like with him."

William Gillette elected to marry him—with consequences that were pleasing to everybody concerned. "I was charmed with the play, the acting, and the pecuniary result," Sir Arthur testified in later years; and for thirty years the public and the box office echoed his applause.

An absurd, preposterous, and thoroughly delightful melodrama, Gillette's *Sherlock Holmes* is possibly the best realization of a novelist's conception ever produced on the stage. With admirable ingenuity the actor-playwright blended some six or seven of the famous tales into a perfect whole, inventing when it was necessary, and created a new adventure that was as fresh and crisp as anything from Watson's notebooks.

Old inhabitants will not forget the Larrabees, that pair of plausible scoundrels, and the strange case of Miss Alice Faulkner. Recovery of the precious "papers" was too perilous a task, however, even for the Larrabees, with Sherlock Holmes on the job—hence Professor Moriarty. He is called Robert in the play, a name unknown to Watson. Incidentally, the original of Moriarty was Adam Worth, who stole the famous Gainsborough in 1876 and hid it for a quarter of a century; this revealed by Sir Arthur in conversation with Dr. Gray Chandler Briggs, whose discovery of the Baker Street digs already has been noted. But even that master criminal might have taken lessons from the Moriarty of Holmes and Watson, a figure of colossal resource and malevolence.

The play opened at the Garrick Theatre, in New York, on November 6, 1899, and ran for 230 performances. Subsequently it played a year on the road, and finally (in 1901) it went to England for a triumphant season at Sir Henry Irving's Lyceum. Since that far time there have been revivals in number, not all of them conducted by Gillette, and the play has been seen in stock. In the detective's role only Gillette is thinkable, if one ardent oldtimer may be permitted to be dogmatic. The original Dr. Watson was the late Bruce McRae, while—charming to recount—an early English "Billy" was a certain Master Charles Chaplin, an orphan boy of talent destined to write his name large in theatrical history.

Chaplin did not play the part in America; but again, in 1905, when Gillette took his *Clarice* to London, Charlie was the dapper "Billy" in a curtain-raiser called *The Painful Predicament of Sherlock Holmes*. King Edward VII, who witnessed the performance at the Duke of York's, read the names of the performers from a program of white satin:

Gwendolyn Cobb .... Miss Irene Vanbrugh
Sherlock Holmes ....Mr. William Gillette
Billy .... Master Charles Chaplin

The skit was a comedy in about one-tenth of an act in which the gaunt detective said precisely nothing at all. The "predicament" involved a young woman of excessive volubility who directed such a passionate stream of words at our hero that he could slip in no word of his own. With the help of Billy, however, he managed to get her out of the house.

Conceivably the greatest triumph of the play was its last revival by Gillette, a victorious occasion. Complicated by sentiment and by historical importance as the situation was, the curious charm of the old play persisted. Oldsters turned out to relive their memories of bygone years, and youngsters to learn what it was their parents had been talking about. And behind it, as always, lay the stupendous legend of Sherlock Holmes, an illusion unique in profane letters. Conan Doyle lived just long enough to congratulate the aging Gillette. "May I add a word to those which are addressed to you on the occasion of your return to the stage?" he wrote. "That this return should be in *Sherlock Holmes* is, of course, a source of personal gratification, my only complaint being that you make the poor hero of the anaemic printed page a very limp object as compared with the glamour of your own personality which you infuse into his stage presentment."

The gratitude of America was expressed by Booth Tarkington in a memorable sentence: "Your return to the stage is a noble and delightful event, and, speaking for myself, I would rather see you play Sherlock Holmes than to be a child again on Christmas morning."

There was no authorized successor to Gillete until 1910, in which year Conan Doyle himself produced a sensational stage version of *The Speckled Band*. His account of it is divertingly set forth in his autobiography, *Memories and Adventures*. Lyn Harding was the formidable Dr. Grimesby Rylott [*sic*] and H. A. Saintsbury was a masterly Sherlock Holmes. Sir Arthur writes:

> We had a fine rock boa to play the title-rôle, a snake which was the pride of my heart, so one can imagine my disgust when I saw that one critic ended his disparaging review with the words, "The crisis of the play was produced by the appearance of a palpably artificial serpent." I was inclined to offer him a goodly sum if he would undertake to go bed with it. We had several snakes at different times, but they were none of them born actors and they were all inclined either to hang down from the hole in the wall like inamimate bell-pulls, or else to turn back through the hole and get even with the stage carpenter who pinched their tails in order to make them more lively. Finally we used artificial snakes and every one, including the stage carpenter, agreed that it was satisfactory.

On the screen the Holmes saga has been prodigiously exploited. Most famous perhaps of motion picture Sherlocks, until the advent of Basil Rathbone, was John Barrymore, who appeared, however, in only one picture.

Clive Brook was also good in one picture, and the only complaint registered against Raymond Massey was that he failed to look Sherlockian. In England there had been Eille Norwood and Arthur Wontner, who looked the part to perfection and turned in sparkling performances; but in America, until the coming of Mr. Rathbone, there had been only one face, Gillette's, to stamp the coinage as authentic. It was the face that Conan Doyle applauded, the face which for the most part illustrators drew, the face with which a world of admiring Watsons was familiar.

Basil Rathbone changed all that. *His*, one supposes, is almost the most familiar male profile of our day. Inevitably he is associated with the role he played so often that he may be said to have made a career of it. He has given us a believable, an unforgettable Holmes, a creation as authentic as that of Gillette, which paradoxically it does not resemble. If, as I like to think, Gillete was born to play the part of Sherlock Holmes, so also was Basil Rathbone. One played him for the nineteenth century, the other for the twentieth.

Spain, France, and Germany (to say nothing of Russia and Japan) have witnessed many Holmes adventures—and almost as many Holmes impersonators—over the years of the detective's greatest popularity. As early as 1905 the Gillette melodrama was playing in Berlin, and a few years later the French version was one of the great successes of the Parisian stage. The French story, indeed, was such a captivating absurdity that it ran for more than 300 performances, and the Parisian police were frequently called on to discourage citizens who imagined themselves to be either Moriartys or incarnations of Sherlock Holmes.

In Spain the popularity of the detective has been at all times enormous. The Iberian imagination reacted warmly to the picturesque fathomer, endowed him with

Spanish qualities and a Spanish caste of countenance, produced endless dime-novel adventures unknown to Watson,[1] and ultimately involved him in combat with celebrated criminals of fiction for whom neither Doyle nor Watson were responsible. His favorite foe on the Spanish stage was the intrepid Raffles, but Arsène Lupin was almost equally popular. A Spanish version of *The Hound of the Baskervilles* offered a delectable bit of stage business that is worth reporting:

> The dog, large and black, with red electric lights for eyes and another to indicate the tongue, is to be mounted on arched crossbows, with paws extended as though running. The crossbows are to be joined by two cross timbers, placed under the feet, and to the foremost cross piece a copper wire is to be attached in such fashion that it may be vigorously pulled to give the animal a galloping movement. Arrangement of the mechanical mounting is to be such that the appliances are not visible from the audience.

Parodists too have taken liberties with Mr. Sherlock Holmes. One of the most humorous libels in my scrapbook is a drawing from an English comic journal. With the utmost consternation depicted on his familiar features, the invincible detective is revealed on a pebbled beach considering the stones that lie around him; apparently there are zillions of them. The text reads simply: "Portrait of a Celebrated Detective Regretting His Rash Decision to Leave No Stone Unturned."

For the most part Sherlockian travesty has been somewhat cruder. Something perhaps of this sort has been a bit more common:

---

[1] In an Armenian novel the great misogynist is revealed as a married man with a largish family.

"Ah, my dear Watson! I see that you have put on your winter underwear."

"Marvelous, Holmes! But how did you deduce it?"

"Elementary, my dear fellow. You have forgotten to put on your trousers!"

Believe me, those lines were not invented for this occasion; they once appeared in several newspapers. Still current, also, is the anecdote of Holmes and a troubled old woman. "I am greatly puzzled, Sir," she tells him. "In one week I have lost a motor horn, a brush, a box of golf balls, a dictionary, and a bootjack. Can you explain it?" "Nothing simpler, Madam," replies the detective. "It is clear that your neighbor keeps a goat."

These specimens of newspaper humor are typical of the sort of burlesque perennially inspired by the Holmes-Watson relationship. It is an easy trick. One would engage to write a dozen similar "comics" in an hour.

Best known to *aficionados,* perhaps, of the more literate parodies is Bret Harte's "The Stolen Cigar Case," a wickedly amusing pastiche. Here are its opening paragraphs

I found Hemlock Jones in the old Brook Street lodgings musing before the fire. With the freedom of an old friend I at once threw myself into my usual familiar attitude at his feet, and gently caressed his boot. . . .

"It is raining," he said, without lifting his head.

"You have been out, then?" I said quickly.

"No. But I see that your umbrella is wet, and that your overcoat has drops of water on it."

I sat aghast at his penetration.

Widely known also are the several travesties by John Kendrick Bangs, now lost in out-of-print volumes. The best of them is *The Pursuit of the Houseboat* (1897), on the dedication page of which one may read:

To A. Conan Doyle, Esq.
With the author's sincerest regards and thanks
for the untimely demise of his great detective
which made these things possible.

The houseboat, it will be remembered, with all its
women on board, had been stolen by Captain Kidd and
his abominable pirates in an earlier volume, *A Houseboat
on the Styx.* Consternation prevailed in Hades, as the
sequel opened, and Lecoq and Hawkshaw were baffled. It
was a newcomer in Hades, a tall and excessively slender
shade—"like a spirt of steam out of a teapot," as Doctor
Johnson put it—who took charge of the pursuit. Captain
Kidd, the newcomer said, had made for London, whither
they must pursue him. He had reached this conclusion
after a devoted study of a cigar stub.

"Your name? your name? cried the Associated
Shades.

The stranger drew forth a bundle of his business cards
and flung them as a prestidigitator tosses aces. They
carried the neatly printed legend:

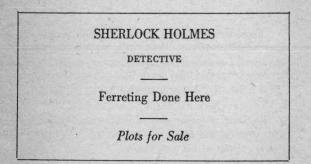

SHERLOCK HOLMES

DETECTIVE

———

Ferreting Done Here

———

Plots for Sale

Mark Twain also had his fun with Sherlock Holmes in
A Double-Barrelled Detective Story; but it is a sad performance, unworthy of its author. Others who have es-
sayed the difficult feat of caricature are James M. Barrie,
A. A. Milne, Harry B. Smith, O. Henry, Robert Barr,

Stephen Leacock, Agatha Christie, Hugh Kingsmill, August Derleth, and the writer of these pages. Among the names given to the long-suffering detective have been such ingenuities as these: Sherlaw Kombs, Picklock Holes, Thinlock Bones, Shylock Homes, Hemlock Jones, Purlock Hone, Holmlock Shears, Herlock Sholmes, Shamrock Jolnes, Sheerluck Hums, Mr. Mycroft, and Solar Pons. We have seen also a Shirley Holmes, a daughter (or perhaps granddaughter) of the Master; and Watson has been variously burlesqued as Whatson, Potson, Whatsoname, Whatsup, Jobson, and Hobson.

One's own favorite among the parodies is Maurice Leblanc's *Arsène Lupin vs. Herlock Sholmes*, surely a monumental compliment in caricature. For what greater compliment could France pay to England, asks T. S. Eliot, than the scene in which the great antagonists, Holmes and Lupin, are lying side by side in deck chairs on the Calais–Dover packet, while the London Commissioner of Police walks up and down before them all unsuspecting?

Stage travesties by intention have been numerous. Most notorious of the lines put into circulation by the actors, perhaps, is the familiar gag, "Quick, Watson, the needle!" Precisely where it originated is still a mystery; but it appeared about the turn of the century in the wake of Gillette's melodrama, which inspired dozens of Holmes-Watson burlesques. Montgomery and Stone may have used it in *The Red Mill*, and undoubtedly T. A. Dorgan spread it across the nation in his sports cartoons in the Hearst newspapers. The line does *not* occur in any of the canonical tales.

Weber and Fields also burlesqued the detective and the doctor, and so did many others. Years ago, in vaudeville, at the old Majestic Theatre in Chicago, I heard the late Lee Harrison intone an amusing ballad, the first stanza and chorus of which proceeded approximately as follows:

I have just arrived from London—
    dear old London, don't you know?—
From my home in Baker Street
    where I've been looking for the dough.
I'm that wonderful detective
    who one night when thinking hard
Found out how many English feet
    there were in Scotland Yard—
I wish Gillette were here;
    he knows me well:
Of my exploits you should hear
    William Tell!

CHORUS:

I can tell the time of day
    by merely looking at a clock;
I can tell you if a street car's going
    up or down the block;
If you'll tell me how old you are
    I'll quickly guess your age;
I can tell an actor every time
    he's riding on a stage!
When a rascally paperhanger
    hung a border on the wall,
I discovered 'twas no boarder—
    just a roomer, that was all!
If your fireplace is defective
Send for me the great detective—
    Mr. Sherlock Holmes is no one else but me!

A lot of water has flowed on the brain since those lines
came across the footlights more than fifty years ago, and
the bibliography of the uncanonical Holmes (or un-
Conanical, as you prefer) is now so extensive as to be
almost forbidding. No one will ever know the number of
advertisers who have seized on Sherlock Holmes for their
own peculiar purposes. The detective has been sponsor,

142

so to speak, for many curious products and, what is worse, incongruous products. Occasionally a clever twist is noted, but for the most part he is caricatured with deerstalker and pipe (sometimes with dog) in pursuit of irrelevant, not to say impertinent, matters. On the whole, the advertisers have been less amusing even than the newspaper humorists. But although large, and perhaps important, the subject is distasteful and uninspiring. Let us be done with it.

The illustrators are another story. Some good men have endeavored to do Holmes justice, and some of them have been notably successful.

The mental image of course is clear. . . . "In height," wrote Watson, in the earliest chronicle, "he was rather over six feet, and so excessively lean that he seemed to be considerably taller. His eyes were sharp and piercing . . . and his thin, hawklike nose gave his whole expression an air of alertness and decision. His chin, too, had the prominence and squareness which mark the man of determination." To this early portrait Sir Arthur Conan Doyle had added: "He had, as I imagined him, a thin razor-like face, with a great hawks-bill of a nose, and two small eyes set close together on either side of it. Such was my conception. It chanced, however, that poor Sidney Paget who, before his premature death, drew all the original pictures, had a younger brother, Walter, who served him as a model. The handsome Walter took the place of the more powerful but uglier Sherlock; and perhaps from the point of view of my lady readers it was as well."

But Sherlock Holmes was too romantic a figure to be a gangling gargoyle even if Sidney Paget's brother had been less of an Adonis. Four illustrators before Paget had tried to depict the saturnine detective, however, and all had botched the task. D. H. Friston was first, although that is about his only distinction. His illustrations for *A*

143

Study in Scarlet, in its first appearance (1887), seem comic to us today; but historically they are important. They contain the first of all the many portraits of Mr. Sherlock Holmes.

In 1888 there was another. Charles Doyle, Sir Arthur's father, was a great and original artist, his son tells us, "more terrible than Blake"; but illustrating books was not his specialty. Charming as it is to possess that *rara avis,* the second edition of *A Study in Scarlet,* it must be conceded that the drawings are pathetic, like the scribblings of a talented child. Nor did Charles Kerr produce a satisfying portrait in 1890, when he was called upon to illustrate the first edition of *The Sign of the Four.* His curious frontispiece depicting Holmes and Watson with the corpse of Bartholomew Sholto is a capable enough bit of melodrama, but one recoils from the idea of a moustached Sherlock.

Thereafter came George Hutchinson, an able draftsman of the *Ally Sloper* school. A series of portraits from his frolic pen illustrates a third edition of the *Study* (1891)—a gallery of caricatures that would have delighted Dickens. For sheer unromantic disillusionment one recommends the portraiture of Hutchinson.

He was followed by Paget, with whom the evolution of the Sherlockian profile may be said to have begun. Later English illustrators for the most part followed Paget, whose first Holmesian [2] drawings were made in 1891 to illustrate the serial appearance of *The Adventures of Sherlock Holmes.* His last pictures illustrated *The Return of Sherlock Holmes* in 1904. For thirteen years his drawings appeared in the *Strand Magazine;* they are part of the legend. It is an interesting circumstance that Walter Paget, the younger brother who was once his model, was called upon to make the pictures for a later Holmes adventure after the elder Paget's death.

---

[2] This word is pronounced *Hol-mesian.*

So much for England. In America there has been really only one illustrator and one portrait from the beginning. Frederic Dorr Steele was not quite the first American artist in the field, but he was incomparably the best. His portrait of Holmes is the established American Sherlock, and it is the acknowledged portrait of William Gillette. Of the thirty-two stories written after 1903, Steele, in his own words, "had the pleasure of illustrating twenty-nine." Perhaps there has been no happier association of author and illustrator since Lewis Carroll and Sir John Tenniel.

It is a popular misconception that Gillette brought to life the illustrations of Frederic Dorr Steele; but the truth is Steele copied the features of the actor. "Everybody agreed that Mr. Gillette was the ideal Sherlock Holmes," said the artist, "and it was inevitable that I should copy him. So I made my models look like him and in some instances used photographs of him in my drawings. But while the actor was seen by thousands, the magazines and books were seen by millions."

Later American illustrators who added to the gallery were Arthur I. Keller, Charles Raymond Macauley, and in the field of caricature, Peter Newell, ablest and most delightful of the comic masters.

All of these, and many more, American and British, are celebrated by James Montgomery in his enchanting album, *A Study in Pictures*, a major contribution to the whole subject of Sherlockiana.

One of the most popular spoofs of Sherlock was told by Sir Arthur Conan Doyle on himself. A Philadelphia cabman greeted him at the station, on his first trip to America—so runs the tale—and "deduced" so much about the visiting stranger and his recent travels that the author was amazed. "How do you do it, my man?" he asked. And the cabman answered: "I looked at the labels pasted on your trunk."

"There is a similar story," writes Conan Doyle in *Memories and Adventures*, "about how Sherlock entered Heaven, and by virtue of his power of observation at once greeted Adam; but the point is perhaps too anatomical for further discussion." [3]

Sherlock Holmes has always been a fair mark for practical jokers, his creator admits:

> I have had numerous bogus cases of various degrees of ingenuity, marked cards, mysterious warnings, cypher messages, and other curious communications. . . . Upon one occasion, as I was entering the hall to take part in an amateur billiard competition, I was handed by the attendant a small packet which had been left for me. Upon opening it I found a piece of ordinary green chalk such as is used in billiards. I was amused by the incident, and I put the chalk into my waistcoat pocket and used it during the game. Afterward, I continued to use it until one day, some months later, as I rubbed the tip of my cue the face of the chalk crumbled in, and I found it was hollow. From the recess thus exposed I drew out a small slip of paper with the words, "From Arsene Lupin to Sherlock Holmes."

Clearly it was a harassed life the great storyteller led, beset at every turn by facetious reminders of his infallible creation. In time he came almost to hate poor Sherlock for obscuring his other literary work, which he believed to be more important than his detective stories. Which just goes to show how wrong a famous writer can be!

---

[3] As told by Dr. Logan Clendening in *The Case of the Missing Patriarchs*, a rare Sherlockian leaflet, Adam was conspicuous because he had no navel.

11

THE

BAKER

STREET

IRREGULARS

And now, gentlemen, in the matter of fictive fathomers, whom will you have? A hulking bully from Headquarters, with a gob of tobacco in his cheek? A lean scientist with high-domed skull, speaking a jargon of the higher mathematics? A dull inspector from the Yard, pursuing his investigations in the stodgy precincts of an English village? A cheeky amateur of unbelievable intuition, with a passion for tea and sausages? Or an amiable dilettante with mismated eyes? Or a blind polyglot, retired? Or a grave professor from the universities? Or Father Brown?

Thank you! I will myself take Mr. Sherlock Holmes of Baker Street. I will take him, if need be, in two handsome omnibus volumes, to a desert island and do without the Bible, the *Iliad,* and Shakespeare.

There are many in the world who feel as I do. On the human side, it is now my duty to report some aspects of the Sherlock Holmes movement in America and the fantastic career of the Baker Street Irregulars. A reprehensible number of us around the nation elect to remain —as far as possible—in the predicament of Walter De la Mare's Jim Jay, who, it will be remembered, got stuck fast in yesterday. We find it comforting in these troubled times to recall the old *Strand Magazine* of the turn of the century, when Sherlock Holmes was adventuring, memoiring, hounding, and returning. . . .

"Let us get back to reality," cried Balzac impatiently to a friend who was boring him with tidings of a sick sister. "Who is going to marry Eugénie Grandet?" And, dying, he murmured: "Bianchon would have saved me!"— referring to the great physician of Paris he had himself created.

That is the way we feel about Sherlock Holmes. Let us be done with all this talk of . . . whatever we may happen to dislike in the daily headlines. Let us speak rather of those things that are permanent and secure, of high matters about which there can be no gibbering division of opinion. Let us speak of the realities that do not change, of that higher realism which is the only true romance. Let us speak, and speak again, of Sherlock Holmes. For the plain fact is, gentlemen, that the imperishable detective—I hope I have said this before—is still a more commanding figure in the world than most of the warriors and statesmen in whose present existence we are invited to believe.

Hence, in part, the Baker Street Irregulars; and hence, perhaps, this book.

The Baker Street Irregulars (as an organization outside the pages of Dr. Watson) were born in the Bowling Green department of the *Saturday Review of Literature*, conducted by Christopher Morley, sometime in 1933. Morley's column had become a meeting place for the Sherlockian wits of the day and ultimately, out of the interest in the Holmes legend fostered by Morley, sprang the BSI. The name was Morley's and no happier one could have been contrived; it captured the imagination of Holmesians around the world. The test for membership became (in 1934) the solution of a crossword puzzle attributed to Inspector Tobias Gregson of Scotland Yard but in fact composed by Frank V. Morley, Christopher Morley's publisher-brother. Charter membership was thus limited at first to some twenty-five or thirty fanatics in New York and a similar number scattered here and there across the nation.

The purpose of the society was the study of the Sacred Writings, i.e., the sixty tales recorded by John H. Watson, M.D. Like other learned and scientific societies, the members exchanged notes of research and contributed "papers" to the general knowledge on such problems as that of the Brothers Moriarty who, it will be recalled, were all named James. This innocent pastime continued throughout 1933 and much of 1934 before the Irregulars became a fact outside the pages of the *Saturday Review*.

The first formal meeting of the group as a public menace was held at Cella's restaurant in New York City on the evening of June 5, 1934, at which time, a high autumnal wind being out of season, every effort was made to create Watson's favorite alternative, an atmosphere of thick yellow fog. Simultaneously the first dinner of the Sherlock Holmes Society of London was going forward in Canuto's restaurant in Baker Street and suitable greetings were exchanged between the celebrating groups. Some months later the honorable secretary of the English society, the Scottish novelist A. G. Macdonell, visited New York and was a guest of honor with William Gillette, the actor, at a second meeting of the BSI on December 7, a happy occasion of both wind and fog.

Possibly an anecdote is in order. To catch the flavor of those early days in the history of the Sherlock Holmes movement—the return to Holmes, as I like to think of it —I must become autobiographical. I had been unable to attend the June meeting, at which the society was tentatively organized, but I journeyed to New York early in December for that first state dinner. In anticipation of a historic event, I wrote to William Gillette inviting him to be my guest and shortly afterward had a note from Alexander Woollcott quizzing me about the affair; so I invited Woollcott also to be my guest, and added that if a hansom cab could be found in New York it would be fitting to charter it for the occasion. This was a notion after his own heart, and more quickly than I had thought possible he wired me that he had rounded up the last two hansoms in the city. They would be at our door on the evening of the dinner, he said.

In due time I reported at Wit's End, Woollcott's apartment in East 52d Street, and found a noisy party in full swing. I supposed he had forgotten the Sherlockian adventure; but nothing could have been farther from the truth. The cocktail party went on to the last possible moment. Then Woollcott prepared to depart, leaving his guests in possession. "The cabs are downstairs, Starrett," he said abruptly. "Come in here a minute."

He dragged me into a bedroom and rapidly outfitted me with a deerstalker cap and a huge reading glass of the sort used by Sherlock Holmes in pictures by illustrators who have no idea what sort of glass Sherlock Holmes used. Thus attired, we descended to the street. The night was unpleasantly cold, there was a hint of fog in the air, and I was bursting with Woollcott's sidecars; but, nightmarishly, at the curb, there really did wait two hansoms, the first of which immediately drove away empty. "Always take the *second* cab," quoted Woollcott, stepping into it. "The first may be dangerous." And to the second driver, urgently, "Follow that cab!"

Thus we set forth. In spite of the weather it was a congested evening in New York; as the two cabs clattered down Fifth Avenue it seemed to me that half the city was abroad to see us pass. Wondering policemen looked hard at the procession but grinned and allowed us to proceed.

Here and there we snarled up traffic briefly; but ultimately, on the tick of the clock—Woollcott had been
making theater curtains that way for years—we de-
bouched on the pavement at Cella's, pushed through a
knot of spectators attracted by our appearance, and
climbed a narrow stairway to an upper room where
another party was in progress. Except that there were no
women present, it looked to me very much like the party
we had just left. A roar went up as we entered in
costume, and then. . . .

Several accounts of this remarkable dinner have been
left to the world and all of them are more plausible than
true. I did not, as Henry Morton Robinson contends,
enter on all fours disguised as the Hound of the Baskervilles; and I did not at any time, as Woollcott records,
read a paper pretending to prove that Sherlock Holmes
was a Cambridge man. I reached the dining room precisely at six-thirty, thanks to Woollcott's uncanny timing,
was greeted by Elmer Davis with a highball in each hand,
and seated myself at the table about seven-thirty, where I
snoozed gently between Morley and Frederic Dorr Steele
—slightly supported by Steele—until perhaps nine. At
that time there was a commotion in the corridor and I
came out of my coma with what novelists describe as a
start. The door was flung swiftly open and in the aperture
stood Sherlock Holmes himself. . . .

It was Gillette of course, and when the uproar had died
away the dinner went forward as planned. My auto-
graphed menu reveals that among those present were
Harold Bell, Basil Davenport, Earle Walbridge, Robert
Keith Leavitt, W. S. Hall, Frank Henry, Malcolm Johnson, Allen Price, Lawrence Dodge, and bluff old Dr. Gray
Chandler Briggs, who had come all the way from St.
Louis to receive the homage due him as the first man to
identify the rooms in Baker Street. It should be said that
ultimately "papers" were read by several of the members and these were later mailed to the membership in

mimeograph so that all might know what had been said at this our eventful first dinner. The menu may be of interest; it reads as follows:

SHERRY NOBLE BACHELOR

•

COCKTAIL MYCROFT

•

PEA SOUP CADOGAN WEST

•

GOOSE HENRY BAKER

•

BROCCOLI COVENT GARDEN

•

CHATEAU REICHENBACH 1891

•

PLOVER'S EGG VIOLET HUNTER

•

FROMAGE MISSING THREE QUARTER

•

BAKED ALASKA DUNDAS

•

CAFE BLACK PETER

•

SCOTCH AND GASOGENE

To return to our irregular history, the original plan of the Irregulars called for an annual dinner on the anniversary of Sherlock's birth, which Morley (with the aid of the stars) had worked out as falling on January 6; but in fact this date is seldom observed. The Baker Street Irregulars, as Morley himself noted, are "too wise to hold stated meetings, which would belie their name and take the fun out of their indoctrinated irregularity." Our "constitution and buy-laws," written by Elmer Davis, is a unique document that readers may care to see in full. Here it is:

CONSTITUTION

ARTICLE I

The name of this society shall be the Baker Street Irregulars.

ARTICLE II

Its purpose shall be the study of the Sacred Writings.

ARTICLE III

All persons shall be eligible for membership who pass an examination in the Sacred Writing set by officers of the society, and who are considered otherwise suitable.

ARTICLE IV

The officers shall be: a Gasogene, a Tantalus, and a Commissionaire.

The duties of the Gasogene shall be those commonly performed by a President.

The duties of the Tantalus shall be those commonly performed by a Secretary.

The duties of the Commissionaire shall be to telephone down for ice, White Rock, and whatever else may be required and available; to conduct all negotiations with waiters; and to assess the members pro rata for the cost of same.

BUY-LAWS

1. An annual meeting shall be held on January 6, at

which the canonical toasts shall be drunk; after which the members shall drink at will.

2. The current round shall be bought by any member who fails to identify, by title of story and context, any quotation from the Sacred Writings submitted by any other member.

Qualification A. If two or more members fail so to identify, a round shall be bought by each of those failing.

Qualification B. If the submitter of the quotation, upon challenge, fails to identify it correctly, he shall buy the round.

3. Special meetings may be called at any time or any place by any one of three members, two of whom shall constitute a quorum.

Qualification A. If said two people are of opposite sexes, they shall use care in selecting the place of meeting, to avoid misinterpretation (or interpretation either, for that matter).

4. All other business shall be left for the monthly meeting.

5. There shall be no monthly meeting.

It was inevitable that scion societies would spring to life in other cities, and this development was not long delayed. Boston, I think, was the first with The Speckled Band and was followed quickly by tight little fellowships in Chicago, San Francisco, Baltimore, Detroit, Indianapolis, and other cities, each aptly named after story titles in the saga. There are now forty or more of these offspring in the field, including half a dozen university chapters. The university chapters are not, as you might recklessly suppose, made up of enthusiastic students; they are made up largely of enthusiastic faculty members. Here is a list of the scion societies as far as they are known to me at this writing::

The Baker Street Irregulars of New York; the Speckled Band of Boston; the Dancing Men of Providence,

R.I.; the Red Circle of Washington, D.C.; the Six Napoleons of Baltimore; the Hounds of the Baskerville *(sic)* of Chicago; the Illustrious Clients of Indianapolis; the Scandalous Bohemians of Akron, Ohio; the Creeping Men of Cleveland; the Amateur Mendicants Society of Detroit; the Sons of the Copper Beeches of Philadelphia; the Scowrers of San Francisco; the Trained Cormorants of Los Angeles; the Musgrave Ritualists of New York; the Diogenes Club of New York; the Diogenes Club of California; the Five Orange Pips of Westchester County, N.Y.; the Priory Scholars of Fordham University; the Greek Interpreters of East Lansing, Mich.; the Briony Lodgers of New York; the Scion of the Four of Morgantown, W. Va.; the Norwegian Explorers of Minneapolis and Saint Paul; the Seventeen Steps of Los Angeles; the Coptic Patriarchs of the University of Chicago; the More Dangerous Crooks of Chicago; the Toronto Squires of Toronto, Ont.; the Puzzling Squires of Columbus; the Bull Pups of Prospect, Ky.; the Wisteria Lodge Confederates of the Eastern Deep South; Hugo's Companions of Chicago; the Canadian Baskervilles; the Boulevard Assassins of Paris; the Crew of the S.S. "Friesland" of Holla. l; Sherlock Holmes Klubben of Denmark; the Baritsu Chapter of Tokyo.

To my knowledge there are only two fellowships that may be called sororities: The Molly McGuires of San Francisco and a distaff scion in Washington, D.C., aptly called The Solitary Cyclist. The Solitary Cyclist is Miss Helene Yuhasova, author of *A Lauriston Garden of Verses,* and poet laureate of the BSI, who meets with herself on unrecorded occasions.

The canonical toasts mentioned in the constitution are offered to Irene Adler, *the* Woman, and the three principals in the Baker Street ménage, the Master, the Doctor, and Mrs. Hudson; but the dramatis personae of the canon is long and various and the opportunities for further toasts are obviously numerous and inspiring.

Meetings are held by the several scion societies more or less at the whim of their officers, some of whom have whimsical titles—I am myself The Needle or presiding officer of the Hounds of the Baskerville (*sic*)—but an annual dinner usually crowns the miscellaneous activities of the year. The spiritual needs of all and sundry are in part supplied by the *Baker Street Journal,* an "irregular quarterly of Sherlockiana," founded by the late Ben Abramson in 1946, with Edgar W. Smith as editor, now also its publisher.[1]

One of the most interesting of the scion societies is the Baritsu Chapter of the BSI, formed in Tokyo (October 12, 1948) by a group of enthusiasts including many of the foreign correspondents then in Japan, as well as several distinguished native Sherlockians. The name derives from the passage in *The Empty House* in which Sherlock Holmes, explaining his return from the dead, attributes his escape from Professor Moriarty to his knowledge of "baritsu, or the Japanese system of wrestling." Unhappily, there is no such word in the Japanese language—or *was* not until October 12, 1948—but Holmes's error has been explained and justified by Count Makino, the distinguished Japanese elder statesman, who was a charter member.

In addition to adding a word to the Japanese language, the Baritsu Chapter erected a plaque on the outer wall of the Criterion Restaurant in London to commemorate the historic meeting of "young Stamford" and Dr. Watson (at the original Criterion Long Bar) which led to the introduction of Dr. Watson to Sherlock Holmes. It was unveiled in Piccadilly on January 3, 1953, by Inspector Robert Fabian of Scotland Yard, but has been missing since the evening of Derby Day, 1956, on which delirious occasion presumably it was pinched by a souvenir

---

[1] The Sherlock Holmes Society of London publishes its own quarterly, the *Sherlock Holmes Journal.*

hunter; at any rate that was the police explanation of the outrage.

More recently (June 25, 1957), the Norwegian Explorers erected a plaque to the Master at the Reichenbachfall, near Meiringen, the scene of Holmes's final meeting with Professor Moriarty, "the Napoleon of Crime, Watson." As far as your chronicler knows, it is still there.

THE FIRST DEPICTION OF THE BAKER STREET IRREGULARS, AS SKETCHED BY CHARLES DOYLE, FATHER OF THE AUTHOR. IT WAS USED IN THE FIRST REPRINT OF *A Study in Scarlet* IN 1888.

12

THE

ADVENTURE OF

THE UNIQUE

"HAMLET"

Being an Unrecorded Adventure of
*Mr. Sherlock Holmes**

1

"Holmes," said I one morning, as I stood in our bay window, looking idly into the street, "surely here comes a madman. Someone has incautiously left the door open and the poor fellow has slipped out. What a pity!"

It was a glorious morning in the spring, with a fresh breeze and inviting sunlight, but as it was early few persons were as yet astir. Birds twittered under the neighboring eaves, and from the far end of the thoroughfare came faintly the droning cry of an umbrella repairman; a lean cat slunk across the cobbles and disappeared into

---

* A pastiche, uncanonical and un-Conanical, and faintly satirical. It may also be read as a good-humored satire on book collectors.

a courtway; but for the most part the street was deserted, save for the eccentric individual who had called forth my exclamation.

Sherlock Holmes rose lazily from the chair in which he had been lounging and came to my side, standing with long legs spread and hands in the pockets of his dressing gown. He smiled as he saw the singular personage coming along; and a personage the man seemed to be, despite his curious actions, for he was tall and portly, with elderly whiskers of the variety called muttonchop, and eminently respectable. He was loping curiously, like a tired hound, lifting his knees high as he ran, and a heavy double watch chain bounced against and rebounded from the plump line of his figured waistcoat. With one hand he clutched despairingly at his tall silk hat, while with the other he made strange gestures in the air, in a state of emotion bordering on distraction. We could almost see the spasmodic workings of his countenance.

"What in the world can ail him?" I cried. "See how he glances at the houses as he passes."

"He is looking at the numbers," responded Sherlock Holmes with dancing eyes, "and I fancy it is ours that will give him the greatest happiness. His profession, of course, is obvious."

"A banker, I should imagine, or at least a person of affluence," I ventured, wondering what curious detail had betrayed the man's vocation to my remarkable companion in a single glance.

"Affluent, yes," said Holmes with a mischievous twinkle, "but not exactly a banker, Watson. Notice the sagging pockets, despite the excellence of his clothing, and the rather exaggerated madness of his eye. He is a collector, or I am very much mistaken."

"My dear fellow!" I exclaimed. "At his age and in his station! And why should he be seeking us? When we settled that last bill——."

"Of books," said my friend severely. "He is a book

collector. His line is Caxtons, Elzevirs, and Gutenberg Bibles, not the sordid reminders of unpaid grocery accounts. See, he is turning in, as I expected, and in a moment he will stand upon our hearthrug and tell the harrowing tale of a unique volume and its extraordinary disappearance."

His eyes gleamed and he rubbed his hands together in satisfaction. I could not but hope that his conjecture was correct, for he had had little recently to occupy his mind, and I lived in constant fear that he would seek that stimulation his active brain required in the long-tabooed cocaine bottle.

As Holmes finished speaking, the doorbell echoed through the house; then hurried feet were sounding on the stairs, while the wailing voice of Mrs. Hudson, raised in protest, could only have been occasioned by frustration of her coveted privilege of bearing up our caller's card. Then the door burst violently inward and the object of our analysis staggered to the center of the room and pitched headforemost upon our center rug. There he lay, a magnificent ruin, with his head on the fringed border and his feet in the coal scuttle; and sealed within his motionless lips was the amazing story he had come to tell —for that it was amazing we could not doubt in the light of our client's extraordinary behavior.

Sherlock Holmes ran quickly for the brandy, while I knelt beside the stricken man and loosened his wilted neckband. He was not dead, and when we had forced the flask beneath his teeth he sat up in groggy fashion, passing a dazed hand across his eyes. Then he scrambled to his feet with an embarrassed apology for his weakness, and fell into the chair which Holmes invitingly held toward him.

"That is right, Mr. Harrington Edwards," said my companion soothingly. "Be quite calm, my dear sir, and when you have recovered your composure you will find us ready to listen."

"You know me then?" cried our visitor. There was pride in his voice and he lifted his eyebrows in surprise.

"I had never heard of you until this moment; but if you wish to conceal your identity it would be well," said Sherlock Holmes, "for you to leave your bookplates at home." As Holmes spoke he returned a little package of folded paper slips, which he had picked from the floor. "They fell from your hat when you had the misfortune to collapse," he added whimsically.

"Yes, yes," cried the collector, a deep blush spreading across his features. "I remember now; my hat was a little large and I folded a number of them and placed them beneath the sweatband. I had forgotten."

"Rather shabby usage for a handsome etched plate," smiled my companion; "but that is your affair. And now, sir, if you are quite at ease, let us hear what it is that has brought you, a collector of books, from Poke Stogis Manor—the name is on the plate—to the office of Sherlock Holmes, consulting expert in crime. Surely nothing but the theft of Mahomet's own copy of the Koran can have affected you so strongly."

Mr. Harrington Edwards smiled feebly at the jest, then sighed. "Alas," he murmured, "if that were all! But I shall begin at the beginning.

"You must know, then, that I am the greatest Shakespearean commentator in the world. My collection of *ana* is unrivaled and much of the world's collection (and consequently its knowledge of the veritable Shakespeare) has emanated from my pen. One book I did not possess: it was unique, in the correct sense of that abused word, the greatest Shakespeare rarity in the world. Few knew that it existed, for its existence was kept a profound secret among a chosen few. Had it become known that this book was in England—anywhere, indeed—its owner would have been hounded to his grave by wealthy Americans.

"It was in the possession of my friend—I tell you this

161

in strictest confidence—of my friend, Sir Nathaniel Brooke-Bannerman, whose place at Walton-on-Walton is next to my own. A scant two hundred yards separate our dwellings; so intimate has been our friendship that a few years ago the fence between our estates was removed, and each of us roamed or loitered at will in the other's preserves.

"For some years, now, I have been at work upon my greatest book—my magnum opus. It was to be my last book also embodying the results of a lifetime of study and research. Sir, I know Elizabethan London better than any man alive; better than any man who ever lived, I think——." He burst suddenly into tears.

"There, there," said Sherlock Holmes gently. "Do not be distressed. Pray continue with your interesting narrative. What was this book—which, I take it, in some manner has disappeared? You borrowed it from your friend?"

"That is what I am coming to," said Mr. Harrington Edwards, drying his tears, "but as for help, Mr. Holmes, I fear ʼ beyond even you. As you surmise, I needed this book. Knowing its value, which could not be fixed, for the book is priceless, and knowing Sir Nathaniel's idolatry of it, I hesitated before asking for the loan of it. But I had to have it, for without it my work could not have been completed, and at length I made my request. I suggested that I visit him and go through the volume under his eyes, he sitting at my side throughout my entire examination, and servants stationed at every door and window, with fowling pieces in their hands.

"You can imagine my astonishment when Sir Nathaniel laughed at my precautions. 'My dear Edwards,' he said, 'that would be all very well were you Arthur Rambidge or Sir Homer Nantes (mentioning the two great men of the British Museum), or were you Mr. Henry Hutterson, the American railway magnate; but you are my friend Harrington Edwards, and you shall take the book home with you for as long as you like.' I protested vigorously, I can assure you; but he would have it so, and as I was touched by this mark of his esteem, at length I permitted him to have his way. My God! If I had remained adamant! If I had only——."

He broke off and for a moment stared blindly into space. His eyes were directed at the Persian slipper on the wall, in the toe of which Holmes kept his tobacco, but we could see that his thoughts were far away.

"Come, Mr. Edwards," said Holmes firmly. "You are agitating yourself unduly. And you are unreasonably prolonging our curiosity. You have not yet told us what this book is."

Mr. Harrington Edwards gripped the arm of the chair in which he sat. Then he spoke, and his voice was low and thrilling.

"The book was a *Hamlet* quarto, dated 1602, presented by Shakespeare to his friend Drayton, with an inscription four lines in length, written and signed by the Master, himself!"

"My dear sir!" I exclaimed. Holmes blew a long, slow whistle of astonishment.

"It is true," cried the collector. "That is the book I borrowed, and that is the book I lost! The long-sought quarto of 1602, actually inscribed in Shakespeare's own hand! His greatest drama, in an edition dated a year earlier than any that is known; a perfect copy, and with four lines in his own handwriting! Unique! Extraordinary! Amazing! Astounding! Colossal! Incredible! Un——."

He seemed wound up to continue indefinitely; but Holmes, who had sat quite still at first, shocked by the importance of the loss, interrupted the flow of adjectives.

"I appreciate your emotion, Mr. Edwards," he said, "and the book is indeed all that you say it is. Indeed, it is so important that we must at once attack the problem of rediscovering it. The book, I take it, is readily indentifiable?"

"Mr. Holmes," said our client, earnestly, "it would be impossible to hide it. It is so important a volume that, upon coming into its possession, Sir Nathaniel Brooke-Bannerman called a consultation of the great binders of the Empire, at which were present Mr. Riviere, Messrs. Sangorski and Sutcliffe, Mr. Zaehnsdorf, and certain others. They and myself, with two others, alone know of the book's existence. When I tell you that it is bound in brown levant morocco, with leather joints and brown levant doublures and flyleaves, the whole elaborately gold-tooled, inlaid with seven hundred and fifty separate pieces of various colored leathers, and enriched by the insertion of eighty-seven precious stones. I need not add that it is a design that never will be duplicated, and I mention only a few of its glories. The binding was personally done by Messrs. Riviere, Sangorski, Sutcliffe, and Zaehnsdorf, working alternately, and is a work of such enchantment that any man might gladly die a thousand deaths for the privilege of owning it for twenty minutes."

"Dear me," quoth Sherlock Holmes, "it must indeed be a handsome volume, and from your description, together with a realization of its importance by reason of its association, I gather that it is something beyond what might be termed a valuable book."

"Priceless!" cried Mr. Harrington Edwards. "The combined wealth of India, Mexico, and Wall Street would be all too little for its purchase."

"You are anxious to recover this book?" asked Sherlock Holmes, looking at him keenly.

"My God!" shrieked the collector, rolling up his eyes and clawing at the air with his hands. "Do you suppose——?"

"Tut, tut!" Holmes interrupted. "I was only teasing you. It is a book that might move even you, Mr. Harrington Edwards, to theft—but we may put aside that notion. Your emotion is too sincere, and besides you know too well the difficulties of hiding such a volume as you describe. Indeed, only a very daring man would purloin it and keep it long in his possession. Pray tell us how you came to lose it."

Mr. Harrington Edwards seized the brandy flask, which stood at his elbow, and drained it at a gulp. With the renewed strength thus obtained, he continued his story:

"As I have said, Sir Nathaniel·forced me to accept the loan of the book, much against my wishes. On the evening that I called for it, he told me that two of his servants, heavily armed, would accompany me across the grounds to my home. 'There is no danger,' he said, 'but you will feel better'; and I heartily agreed with him. How shall I tell you what happened? Mr. Holmes, it was those very servants who assailed me and robbed me of my priceless borrowing!"

Sherlock Holmes rubbed his lean hands with satisfaction. "Splendid!" he murmured. "This is a case after my own heart. Watson, these are deep waters in which we are adventuring. But you are rather lengthy about this, Mr. Edwards. Perhaps it will help matters if I ask you a few questions. By what road did you go to your home?"

"By the main road, a good highway which lies in front of our estates. I preferred it to the shadows of the wood."

"And there were some two hundred yards between your doors. At what point did the assault occur?"

"Almost midway between the two entrance drives, I should say."

"There was no light?"

"That of the moon only."

"Did you know these servants who accompanied you?"

"One I knew slightly; the other I had not seen before."

"Describe them to me, please."

"The man who is known to me is called Miles. He is

clean-shaven, short and powerful, although somewhat elderly. He was known, I believe, as Sir Nathaniel's most trusted servant; he had been with Sir Nathaniel for years. I cannot describe him minutely for, of course, I never paid much attention to him. The other was tall and thickset, and wore a heavy beard. He was a silent fellow; I do not believe that he spoke a word during the journey."

"Miles was more communicative?"

"Oh yes—even garrulous, perhaps. He talked about the weather and the moon, and I forget what else."

"Never about books?"

"There was no mention of books between any of us."

"Just how did the attack occur?"

"It was very sudden. We had reached, as I say, about the halfway point, when the big man seized me by the throat—to prevent outcry, I suppose—and on the instant, Miles snatched the volume from my grasp and was off. In a moment his companion followed him. I had been half throttled and could not immediately cry out; but when I could articulate, I made the countryside ring with my cries. I ran after them, but failed even to catch another sight of them. They had disappeared completely."

"Did you all leave the house together?"

"Miles and I left together; the second man joined us at the porter's lodge. He had been attending to some of his duties."

"And Sir Nathaniel—where was he?"

"He said good-night on the threshold."

"What has he had to say about all this?"

"I have not told him."

"You have not told him?" echoed Sherlock Holmes, in astonishment.

"I have not dared," confessed our client miserably. "It will kill him. That book was the breath of his life."

"When did all this occur?" I put in, with a glance at Holmes.

"Excellent, Watson," said my friend, answering my glance. "I was just about to ask the same question."

"Just last night," was Mr. Harrington Edwards' reply. "I was crazy most of the night, and didn't sleep a wink. I came to you the first thing this morning. Indeed, I tried to raise you on the telephone, last night, but could not establish a connection."

"Yes," said Holmes, reminiscently, "we were attending Mme Trentini's first night. We dined later at Albani's."

"Oh, Mr. Holmes, do you think you can help me?" cried the abject collector.

"I trust so," answered my friend, cheerfully. "Indeed, I am certain I can. Such a book, as you remark, is not easily hidden. What say you, Watson, to a run down to Walton-on-Walton?"

"There is a train in half an hour," said Mr. Harrington Edwards, looking at his watch. "Will you return with me?"

"No, no," laughed Holmes, "that would never do. We must not be seen together just yet, Mr. Edwards. Go back yourself on the first train, by all means, unless you have further business in London. My friend and I will go together. There is another train this morning?"

"An hour later."

"Excellent. Until we meet, then!"

2

We took the train from Paddington Station an hour later, as we had promised, and began our journey to Walton-on-Walton, a pleasant, aristocratic little village and the scene of the curious accident to our friend of Poke Stogis Manor. Sherlock Holmes, lying back in his seat, blew earnest smoke rings at the ceiling of our compartment, which fortunately was empty, while I devoted myself to the morning paper. After a bit I tired of this occupation and turned to Holmes to find him looking out of the window, wreathed in smiles, and quoting Horace softly under his breath.

"You have a theory?" I asked, in surprise.

"It is a capital mistake to theorize in advance of the evidence," he replied. "Still, I have given some thought to the interesting problem of our friend, Mr. Harrington Edwards, and there are several indications which can point to only one conclusion."

"And whom do you believe to be the thief?"

"My dear fellow," said Sherlock Holmes, "you forget we already know the thief. Edwards has testified quite clearly that it was Miles who snatched the volume."

"True," I admitted, abashed. "I had forgotten. All we must do then, is to find Miles."

"And a motive," added my friend, chuckling. "What would you say, Watson, was the motive in this case?"

"Jealousy," I replied.

"You surprise me!"

"Miles had been bribed by a rival collector, who in some manner had learned about this remarkable volume. You remember Edwards told us this second man joined them at the lodge. That would give an excellent opportunity for the substitution of a man other than the servant intended by Sir Nathaniel. Is not that good reasoning?"

"You surpass yourself, my dear Watson," murmured Holmes. "It is excellently reasoned, and as you justly observe, the opportunity for a substitution was perfect."

"Do you not agree with me?"

"Hardly, Watson. A rival collector, in order to accomplish this remarkable coup, first would have to have known of the volume, as you suggest, but also he must have known upon what night Mr. Harrington Edwards would go to Sir Nathaniel's to get it, which would point to collaboration on the part of our client. As a matter of fact, however, Mr. Edwards' decision to accept the loan

168

was, I believe, sudden and without previous determination."

"I do not recall his saying so."

"He did not say so, but it is a simple deduction. A book collector is mad enough to begin with, Watson; but tempt him with some such bait as this Shakespeare quarto and he is bereft of all sanity. Mr. Edwards would not have been able to wait. It was just the night before that Sir Nathaniel promised him the book, and it was just last night that he flew to accept the offer—flying, incidentally, to disaster also. The miracle is that he was able to wait an entire day."

"Wonderful!" I cried.

"Elementary," said Holmes. "If you are interested, you will do well to read Harley Graham on *Transcendental Emotion;* while I have myself been guilty of a small brochure in which I catalogue some twelve hundred professions and the emotional effect upon their members of unusual tidings, good and bad."

We were the only passengers to alight at Walton-on-Walton, but rapid inquiry developed that Mr. Harrington Edwards had returned on the previous train. Holmes, who had disguised himself before leaving the coach, did all the talking. He wore his cap peak backward, carried a pencil behind his ear, and had turned up the bottoms of his trousers; while from one pocket dangled the end of a linen tape measure. He was a municipal surveyor to the life, and I could not but think that, meeting him suddenly in the highway I should not myself have known him. At his suggestion, I dented the crown of my hat and turned my jacket inside out. Then he gave me an end of the tape measure, while he, carrying the other, went on ahead. In this fashion, stopping from time to time to kneel in the dust and ostensibly to measure sections of the roadway, we proceeded toward Poke Stogis Manor. The occasional villagers whom we encountered on their way to the station paid us no more attention than if we had been rabbits.

Shortly we came in sight of our friend's dwelling, a picturesque and rambling abode, sitting far back in its own grounds and bordered by a square of sentinel oaks. A gravel pathway led from the roadway to the house entrance and, as we passed, the sunlight struck fire from an antique brass knocker on the door. The whole picture, with its background of gleaming countryside, was one of rural calm and comfort; we could with difficulty believe it the scene of the curious problem we had come to investigate.

We shall not enter yet," said Sherlock Holmes, passing the gate leading into our client's acreage; "but we shall endeavor to be back in time for luncheon."

From this point the road progressed downward in a gentle decline and the vegetation grew more thickly on either side of the road. Sherlock Holmes kept his eyes stolidly on the path before us, and when we had covered about a hundred yards he stopped. "Here," he said, pointing, "the assault occurred."

I looked closely at the earth, but could see no sign of struggle.

"You recall it was midway between the two houses that it happened," he continued. "No, there are few signs; there was no violent tussle. Fortunately, however, we had our proverbial fall of rain last evening and the earth has retained impressions nicely." He indicated the faint imprint of a foot, then another, and still another. Kneeling down, I was able to see that, indeed, many feet had passed along the road.

Holmes flung himself at full length in the dirt and wriggled swiftly about, his nose to the earth, muttering rapidly in French. Then he whipped out a glass, the better to examine something that had caught his eye; but in a moment he shook his head in disappointment and continued with his exploration. I was irresistibly reminded of a noble hound, at fault, sniffing in circles in an effort to re-establish a lost scent. In a moment, however, he had it, for with a little cry of pleasure he rose to his feet, zigzagged curiously across the road and paused before a bridge, a lean finger pointing accusingly at a break in the thicket.

"No wonder they disappeared," he smiled as I came up. "Edwards thought they continued up the road, but here is where they broke through." Then stepping back a little distance, he ran forward lightly and cleared the hedge at a bound.

"Follow me carefully," he warned, "for we must not allow our own footprints to confuse us." I fell more heavily than my companion, but in a moment he had me up and helped me to steady myself. "See," he cried, examining the earth; and deep in the mud and grass I saw the prints of two pairs of feet.

"The small man broke through," said Sherlock Holmes, exultantly, "but the larger rascal leaped over the hedge. See how deeply his prints are marked; he landed heavily here in the soft ooze. It is significant, Watson, that they came this way. Does it suggest nothing to you?"

"That they were men who knew Edwards' grounds as well as the Brooke-Bannerman estate," I answered; and thrilled with pleasure at my friend's nod of approbation.

He flung himself upon the ground without further conversation, and for some moments we both crawled painfully across the grass. Then a shocking thought occurred to me.

"Holmes," I whispered in dismay, "do you see where these footprints tend? They are directed toward the home of our client, Mr. Harrington Edwards!"

He nodded his head slowly, and his lips were tight and thin. The double line of impressions ended abruptly at the back door of Poke Stogis Manor!

Sherlock Holmes rose to his feet and looked at his watch.

"We are just in time for luncheon," he announced, and brushed off his garments. Then, deliberately, he knocked upon the door. In a few moments we were in the presence of our client.

"We have been roaming about in the neighborhood," apologized the detective, "and took the liberty of coming to your rear door."

"You have a clue?" asked Mr. Harrington Edwards eagerly.

A queer smile of triumph sat upon Holmes's lips.

"Indeed," he said quietly, "I believe I have solved your little problem, Mr. Harrington Edwards."

"My dear Holmes!" I cried, and "My dear sir!" cried our client.

"I have yet to establish a motive," confessed my friend; "but as to the main facts there can be no question."

Mr. Harrington Edwards fell into a chair; he was white and shaking.

"The book," he croaked. "Tell me."

"Patience, my good sir," counseled Holmes kindly. "We have had nothing to eat since su up, and we are famished. All in good time. Let us fi have luncheon and then all shall be made clear. Meanwhile, I should like to telephone to Sir Nathaniel Brooke-Bannerman, for I wish him also to hear what I have to say."

Our client's pleas were in vain. Holmes would have his little joke and his luncheon. In the end, Mr. Harrington Edwards staggered away to the kitchen to order a repast, and Sherlock Holmes talked rapidly and unintelligibly into the telephone and came back with a smile on his face. But I asked no questions; in good time this extraordinary man would tell his story in his own way. I had heard all that he had heard, and had seen all that he had seen; yet I was completely at sea. Still, our host's ghastly smile hung heavily in my mind, and come what would I felt sorry for him. In a little time we were seated at table. Our client, haggard and nervous, ate slowly and with apparent discomfort; his eyes were never long absent from Holmes's inscrutable face. I was little better off, but Sherlock Holmes ate with gusto, relating meanwhile a number of his earlier adventures—which I may some day give to the world, if I am able to read my illegible notes made on the occasion.

When the dreary meal had been concluded we went into the library, where Sherlock Holmes took possession of the easiest chair with an air of proprietorship that would have been amusing in other circumstances. He screwed together his long pipe and lighted it with almost malicious lack of haste, while Mr. Harrington Edwards perspired against the mantel in an agony of apprehension.

"Why must you keep us waiting, Mr. Holmes?" he whispered. "Tell us, at once, please, who—— who——." His voice trailed off into a moan.

"The criminal," said Sherlock Holmes smoothly, "is——."

"Sir Nathaniel Brooke-Bannerman!" said a maid, suddenly putting her head in at the door; and on the heels of her announcement stalked the handsome baronet, whose priceless volume had caused all this commotion and unhappiness.

Sir Nathaniel was white, and he appeared ill. He burst at once into talk.

"I have been much upset by your call," he said, looking meanwhile at our client. "You say you have something to tell me about the quarto. Don't say—— that—— anything—— has happened—— to it!" He clutched nervously at the wall to steady himself, and I felt deep pity for the unhappy man.

Mr. Harrington Edwards looked at Sherlock Holmes. "Oh, Mr. Holmes," he cried pathetically, "why did you send for him?"

"Because," said my friend, "I wish him to hear the

173

truth about the Shakespeare quarto. Sir Nathaniel, I be-lieve you have not been told as yet that Mr. Edwards was robbed, last night, of your precious volume—robbed by the trusted servants whom you sent with him to protect it."

"What!" screamed the titled collector. He staggered and fumbled madly at his heart, then collapsed into a chair. "My God!" he muttered, and then again: "My God!"

"I should have thought you would have been suspicious of evil when your servants did not return," pursued the detective.

"I have not seen them," whispered Sir Nathaniel. "I do not mingle with my servants. I did not know they had failed to return. Tell me—— tell me all!"

"Mr. Edwards," said Sherlock Holmes, turning to our client, "will you repeat your story, please?"

Mr. Harrington Edwards, thus adjured, told the un-happy tale again, ending with a heartbroken cry of "Oh, Nathaniel, can you ever forgive me?"

"I do not know that it was entirely your fault," observed Holmes cheerfully. "Sir Nathaniel's own servants are the guilty ones, and surely he sent them with you."

"But you said you had solved the case, Mr. Holmes," cried our client, in a frenzy of despair.

"Yes," agreed Holmes, "it is solved. You have had the clue in your own hands ever since the occurrence, but you did not know how to use it. It all turns upon the curious actions of the taller servant, prior to the assault."

"The actions of——?" stammered Mr. Harrington Edwards. "Why, he did nothing—— said nothing!"

"That is the curious circumstance," said Sherlock Holmes. Sir Nathaniel got to his feet with difficulty.

"Mr. Holmes," he said, "this has upset me more than I can tell you. Spare no pains to recover the book and to bring to justice the scoundrels who stole it. But I must go away and think—— think——."

"Stay," said my friend. "I have already caught one of them."

"What! Where?" cried the two collectors together.

"Here," said Sherlock Holmes, and stepping forward he laid a hand on the baronet's shoulder. "You, Sir Nathaniel, were the taller servant, you were one of the thieves who throttled Mr. Harrington Edwards and took from him your own book. And now, sir, will you tell us why you did it?"

Sir Nathaniel Brooke-Bannerman staggered and would have fallen had not I rushed forward and supported him. I placed him in a chair. As we looked at him we saw confession in his eyes; guilt was written in his haggard face.

"Come, come," said Holmes impatiently. "Or will it make it easier for you if I tell the story as it occurred? Let it be so, then. You parted with Mr. Harrington Edwards on your doorsill, Sir Nathaniel, bidding your best friend good-night with a smile on your lips and evil in your heart. And as soon as you had crossed the door, you slipped into an enveloping raincoat, turned up your collar, and hastened by a shorter road to the porter's lodge, where you joined Mr. Edwards and Miles as one of your own servants. You spoke no word at any time, because you feared to speak. You were afraid Mr. Edwards would recognize your voice, while your beard, hastily assumed, protected your face and in the darkness your figure passed unnoticed.

"Having strangled and robbed your best friend, then, of your own book, you and your scoundrelly assistant fled across Mr. Edwards' fields to his own back door, thinking that, if investigation followed, I would be called in, and would trace those footprints and fix the crime upon Mr. Harrington Edwards—as part of a criminal plan, prearranged with your rascally servants, who would be supposed to be in the pay of Mr. Edwards and the ringleaders in a counterfeit assault upon his person. Your mistake, sir, was in ending your trail abruptly at Mr. Edwards' back door. Had you left another trail, then, leading back to your own domicile, I should unhesitatingly have arrested Mr. Harrington Edwards for the theft.

"Surely you must know that in criminal cases handled by me, it is never the obvious solution that is the correct one. The mere fact that the finger of suspicion is made to point at a certain individual is sufficient to absolve that individual from guilt. Had you read the little works of my friend and colleague, Dr. Watson, you would not have made such a mistake. Yet you claim to be a bookman!"

A low moan from the unhappy baronet was his only answer.

"To continue, however; there at Mr. Edwards' own back door you ended your trail, entering his house—his own house—and spending the night under his roof, while his cries and ravings over his loss filled the night and brought joy to your unspeakable soul. And in the morning, when he had gone forth to consult me, you quietly left—you and Miles—and returned to your own place by the beaten highway."

"Mercy!" cried the defeated wretch, cowering in his chair. "If it is made public, I am ruined. I was driven to it. I could not let Mr. Edwards examine the book, for that way exposure would follow; yet I could not refuse him—my best friend—when he asked its loan."

"Your words tell me all that I did not know," said Sherlock Holmes sternly. "The motive now is only too plain. The work, sir, was a forgery, and knowing that your erudite friend would discover it, you chose to blacken his name to save your own. Was the book insured?"

"Insured for £100,000, he told me," interrupted Mr. Harrington Edwards excitedly.

"So that he planned at once to dispose of this dangerous and dubious item, and to reap a golden reward," commented Holmes. "Come, sir, tell us about it. How much of it was forgery? Merely the inscription?"

"I will tell you," said the baronet suddenly, "and throw myself upon the mercy of my friend, Mr. Edwards. The whole book, in effect, was a forgery. It was originally made up of two imperfect copies of the 1604 quarto. Out of the pair I made one perfect volume, and a skillful workman, now dead, changed the date for me so cleverly that only an expert of the first water could have detected it. Such an expert, however, is Mr. Harrington Edwards —the one man in the world who could have unmasked me."

"Thank you, Nathaniel," said Mr. Harrington Edwards gratefully.

"The inscription, of course, also was forged," continued the baronet. "You may as well know everything."

"And the book?" asked Holmes. "Where did you destroy it?"

A grim smile settled on Sir Nathaniel's features. "It is even now burning in Mr. Edwards' own furnace," he said.

"Then it cannot yet be consumed," cried Holmes, and dashed into the cellar, to ᴇᴍᴇʀge some moments later, in high spirits, carrying a charred leaf of paper in his hand.

"It is a pity," he cried, "a pity! In spite of its questionable authenticity, it was a noble specimen. It is only half consumed; but let it burn away. I have preserved one leaf as a souvenir of the occasion." He folded it carefully and placed it in his wallet. "Mr. Harrington Edwards, I fancy the decision in this matter is for you to announce. Sir Nathaniel, of course, must make no effort to collect the insurance."

"Let us forget it, then," said Mr. Harrington Edwards, with a sigh. "Let it be a sealed chapter in the history of bibliomania." He looked at Sir Nathaniel Brooke-Bannerman for a long moment, then held out his hand. "I forgive you, Nathaniel," he said simply.

Their hands met; tears stood in the baronet's eyes.

Powerfully moved, Holmes and I turned from the affecting scene and crept to the door unnoticed. In a moment the free air was blowing on our temples, and we were coughing the dust of the library from our lungs.

3

"They are a strange people, these book collectors," mused Sherlock Holmes as we rattled back to town.

"My only regret is that I shall be unable to publish my notes on this interesting case," I responded.

"Wait a bit, my dear Doctor," counseled Holmes, "and it will be possible. In time both of them will come to look upon it as a hugely diverting episode, and will tell it upon themselves. Then your notes shall be brought forth and the history of another of Mr. Sherlock Holmes's little problems shall be given to the world."

"It will always be a reflection upon Sir Nathaniel," I demurred.

"He will glory in it," prophesied Sherlock Holmes. "He will go down in bookish circles with Chatterton, and Ireland, and Payne Collier. Mark my words, he is not blind even now to the chance this gives him for a sinister immortality. He will be the first to tell it."

"But why did you preserve the leaf from *Hamlet?*" I inquired. "Why not a jewel from the binding?"

Sherlock Holmes laughed heartily. Then he slowly unfolded the leaf in question, and directed a humorous finger to a spot upon the page.

"A fancy," he responded, "to preserve so accurate a characterization of either of our friends. The line is a real jewel. See, the good Polonius says: 'That he is mad, 'tis true; 'tis true 'tis pittie; and pittie 'tis 'tis true.' There is as much sense in Master Will as in Hafiz or Confucius, and a greater felicity of expression. . . . Here is London, and now, my dear Watson, if we hasten we shall be just in time for Zabriski's matinee!"

AVE

SHERLOCK

Some years ago the late Robert Ripley, writing of the "seven most interesting thoroughfares in the world," listed them as follows: Ghat of the Ganges (Benares), Bubbling Well Road (Shanghai), Broadway at Night (New York), the Street of David (Jerusalem), Calle Florida (Buenos Aires), the Champs-Elysées (Paris), Tala (Fez). The late Burton Holmes, given opportunity, might have added the Street of the Café de la Paix, in Paris, since this to him was the center of the universe. Thomas Burke, I think, might conceivably have named first some opium-drenched alley in Limehouse.

But surely for armies of readers the most interesting street in the world is London's Baker Street, forever the address of Sherlock Holmes and Dr. Watson. A drab street now, cold and inhospitable to the eye; a London fog in brick and stone; yet a street that the heart remembers when others are forgotten. A street of ghosts, if you will; but how persuasive the discarnate tread on the seventeen steps that lead upward to those memorable rooms. If there be one person yet living who questions the reality of these wraiths, let him write to the Central Post Office, London, and ask how many letters have been received in the last half century addressed to Mr. Sherlock Holmes at No. 221B Baker Street—a man (cynics will tell you) who never lived and a house that never existed. But the house in Baker Street still stands. It will continue to stand as long as the cold London fog rolls in with the winter and mischief is planned and thwarted and books are written and read.

"ELEMENTARY, MY DEAR WATSON!" FREDERIC DORR STEELE'S MOST FAMOUS SKETCH OF THE MASTER SLEUTH.

THE PRIVATE

LIFE OF

VINCENT

STARRETT

by Michael Murphy

This brief survey of the life of Vincent Starrett was written at the time of his death on January 5, 1974, for delivery as a eulogy on January 9, 1974. It was published by Pontine Press in a limited edition of 400 copies in October, 1974, along with the words and order of the funeral service conducted for Vincent Starrett. It is here reprinted for the first time, with the kind permission of Luther Norris, editor and publisher of the Pontine Press.

The author of *The Private Life of Sherlock Holmes* had his own private life, and his own public life, both of which were fascinating on their respective levels, in their varied adventures and associations, in their searching voyages on the rocky seas of finely charted scholarship, and in their many fulfillments.

The younger, adventurous Starrett was an intriguing person, for his curiosity was constant and unrestricted, his courage was reckless and sustained, and his many enthusiasms in both life and letters were freely and vibrantly expressed. In the following pages the reader who knows Starrett's work will learn more about his life; and the reader who is not yet familiar with his work will find that it is an enlightening view of one of the great writers of the twentieth century.

A report of the death of Vincent Starrett appeared in a British journal in 1973. But that was not the last report, nor the first. One of the earlier, mysterious rumors of Starrett's death circulated back in the '40s. That was when Joseph Kelly Vodrey of the Brush-Moore newspapers in Ohio sent his condolences to Colonel Robert McCormick of the *Tribune*. "With Starrett's death," Vodrey wrote, "the *Tribune* has lost not only one of its great book columnists, but one of the finest newspapermen of all time."

The colonel had a vague recollection of having passed Starrett in the hall only a day or two before. Was it possible that Starrett was really dead? The colonel sent out a rash of inquiries, and in due course Starrett materialized as irrefutable evidence that he was alive and well. Starrett insisted, moreover, that unless the story of his death could be verified, he should be kept on the payroll.

But no, that was not the last report of Starrett's death.

There were the other, even earlier reports: the one, for example, that came out of Mexico in 1914. Starrett had been shot to death by Zapatistas at the still-unrecorded battle of Xochimilco. Well, it was true that he had been shot, but it was only a leg wound, and the battle had been more legendary than true, largely a hoax perpetrated by the war correspondents to make some copy. That report, then, like the others, was not the last report of Starrett's death.

The earliest report, I suspect, was the one on which Starrett himself commented in both his autobiography and one of his novels: that incident goes back to his birth in Toronto on October 26, 1886. He had been born dead, the physician concluded, and he wrapped the infant in the daily newspaper and placed him under the bed. Eventually, the newborn's cries alerted them to his living presence. Starrett later commented that "none of my writing colleagues can boast of an earlier appearance in print."

But that, after all, was the earliest, not the latest, report of Starrett's death. There was the report that Starrett had died on January 5, 1974, at 12:15 P.M. at St. Anthony's Hospital in Chicago. That was the last report; it is the only true report of the death of Vincent Starrett that was ever issued.

Vincent Starrett was eighty-seven when he died. In those eighty-seven years, he published more than 200 books and pamphlets, and perhaps as many as 500 articles and stories. He also attended two wars, married two women, exhumed several great writers, and lived in China, Mexico, London, Paris, and cities throughout the United States. He loved Chicago. He was a part of the city, and the city was a part of him. He wrote about it as it was in the days he knew it, as it was in the days others knew it. There were times in the city of Chicago that cannot be written about without mentioning Vincent Starrett. He was part of the times. And, in his timeless way, he was the definition of every period of civilized man.

Starrett's newspaper career began on the old Chicago *Inter-Ocean* in 1907. He was twenty years old then, and his writing career had begun, in effect, sixteen years before, in Toronto. The opportunity to become both a well-read man and a widely read writer fell to him quite providentially, because his mother was a schoolteacher and a writer, and his grandfather was a bookseller.

Most of Starrett's school vacations, after he left Toronto for Chicago, were spent back in the city of his birth, and much of his time was devoted to reading the books in his grandfather's shop. From the age of four to fourteen, Starrett read more books than most highly literate people read in a lifetime.

His earliest recollection of Chicago involved a dingy flat on Van Buren Street near Loomis, a cigar-store Indian called Rain-in-the-Face, the Moody Bible Institute, where he heard the famous Dwight Moody speak, and the World's Columbian Exposition of 1893.

His early schooling was at John Ericsson grammar school in Chicago. Prior to being graduated in 1899, he earned the silver medal awarded for the best essay on patriotism written by an eighth-grader. He remembered, in later years, the opening words of that essay: "A crisis in the affairs of a nation always brings forth men who rise to meet the occasion. There are in every land men who are so filled with love of country that they are willing to sacrifice even life itself to serve the country's best interests."

He said it was one of the best essays his mother ever wrote.

He wrote hundreds of his own, however, in other years, including some of the finest literary essays in the English language. Early influences in this direction can be identified at John Marshall High School, where he had not only an encouraging English teacher but a school principal who was himself a writer. Starrett's first published piece in the high school literary paper was a poem inspired by the death of Queen Victoria. "The Queen has passed to the unknown, no other had such fame, King Edward reigns on England's throne, the seventh of his name. Mourned as a woman and a queen, the fairest of her race, down through the ages rings the paean of her immortal grace."

Starrett's teacher and the school principal both predicted a brilliant writing career for him, and he fulfilled their prophecy while they were still alive. After he was graduated from high school in 1904, he had an adventure in London, on his own, but failed to find enduring employment as a London journalist. On his return to Chicago, he worked at a diversity of jobs for a brief period before settling in the newspaper field. "In those early years of the new century," he wrote, "Chicago was an interesting and exciting place. Transportation was beginning to be mechanized, the change had been in progress for some time; but there were still horses in the street and the automobile was still a novelty."

In 1906 there were seven papers in Chicago, the *Tribune*, the *Daily News*, the *Inter-Ocean*, the *Record-Herald*, the *Journal*, the *Evening Post*, and the *Dispatch*. Starrett was hired by the *Inter-Ocean* and worked the first two weeks without pay; he was then given twelve dollars a week for the eleven months he remained with the paper. It was at the *Inter-Ocean* that he gained much valuable journalistic experience and met some of the famous editors and writers who were later celebrated in the Hecht-MacArthur *The Front Page*. He also worked with Ring and Rex Lardner, Burns Mantle, H. T. Webster and other notable newsmen, writers and cartoonists.

His story of his first police assignment as a cub reporter is memorable, in that it was a murder case where a butcher had used his cleaver to hack off his wife's head. Starrett was assigned to photograph the butcher, his wife, and the family. He arrived at the scene of the crime and, getting no answer to his knocking, crawled through a window, stumbling to a bed on which, to his horror, the body of the victim lay, "clad only in her gore, the severed head and body reunited, an appreciable gap between . . ."

This lesson was not effective or lasting, for shortly after, Starrett crawled through another window on another murder story in which an entire family had been poisoned. He was snatching photographs from the mantelpiece when he heard the steps of someone else. He came face to face with the unknown in the darkness, only to discover that it was another crime reporter from his own paper, who had also crawled through the window seeking clues.

Starrett's contact with reality through his newspaper training stilled his literary ambitions for a time, and he went from the *Inter-Ocean* to the *Daily News* at an increase of seven dollars a week. The city room of the *News* overlooked the "L" platform on Wells Street, which was then called Fifth Avenue, and it was in Starrett's words, "warm and friendly and, to a romantic newcomer, as full of drama and suspense as a detective novel." Henry Justin Smith of the *News* was the great editor in Starrett's experience, the one who influenced him most, and Starrett is one of the minor celebrities in Smith's book *Deadlines*. Some of the others who worked with Starrett on the *News* were Ben Hecht, Wallace Smith, Harry Hansen, Junius Wood, Keith Preston, John Gunther, Robert Casey, Carl Sandburg, and Howard Vincent O'Brien.

One of Starrett's influential feature stories at the time derived from his visit to a maternity hospital. He learned that babies were sometimes given to childless and barren women who palmed them off to their husbands as their own. This story created an uproar, and in time resulted in a successful theatrical comedy by Margaret Mayo called *Baby Mine*.

Starrett's journalistic career flourished after a fashion and in 1909 he was given a raise to twenty-five dollars a week, a sufficient encouragement for him to marry a redhaired piano player named Lillian Hartsig. The assistant city editor on the *News* commented, "Poor old Starrett—he'll never again lie diagonally in bed."

In his role as reporter, he met a good many celebrities, but he cherished memories of these less than the late afternoon "dog watches" at the paper, when he and the other news writers with literary ambitions toiled away on their private little masterpieces. It was in 1914 that

186

Starrett and Hecht got together, and it is only fair to say that Hecht was a hard-working writer, and equally proper to name Starrett as a very dominant influence in what Hecht was writing and reading. Burton Rascoe said that Starrett was responsible for educating the entire city room, a charge that Starrett modestly denied, admitting only to the fact that he directed a number of his writing colleagues to books they had never read before.

This was one of Starrett's professional roles in the literary world as well as in the local room; indeed, it was around this time that he began to read and write about those relatively neglected authors who were to enjoy within the following decade enthusiastic revivals. Starrett introduced Hecht and others to the works of Arthur Machen, Stephen Crane, Ambrose Bierce, and Haldane MacFall. All of these writers had fallen into neglect, and one of them, Machen, had not even been published in the United States.

One of the famous stories of Starrett's association with Hecht related to the Ouija board that Hecht had brought into the office one afternoon. Hecht had succeeded in communicating with the ghost of a man named Wilson, from whom he had elicited a great deal of information. One day Hecht asked Starrett what was the most valuable book in the world, and Starrett replied, "Poe's *Tamerlane*," whereupon Hecht asked Mr. Wilson thru the instrument of the Ouija where a copy of the book might be found. The Ouija, or Mr. Wilson, gave them the initials J. A. N. "Jan!" Hecht exclaimed. "Do you know anybody named Jan?"

Starrett thought momentarily and then identified a bookseller on Adams Street whose name was Jansky.

The Ouija confirmed that Jansky *was* the party all right, and even went so far as to tell them that the rare Poe volume could be found in the ten-cent bin outside Jansky's door.

Starrett and Hecht proceeded to Jansky's and spent

about an hour on their hands and knees, looking for the rare Poe volume. Unfortunately, it did not turn up.

Hecht and Starrett communicated with Mr. Wilson only sparingly after that.

Starrett's dream, in addition to that of gaining fame as a writer, was to serve as a war correspondent. The dream came true when he and Junius Wood were ordered by the *Daily News* to cover the Mexican conflict in 1914. Starrett was assigned to the Fifth Brigade under General Funston. One of the joys of his assignment was the opportunity it gave him to become a good friend to both Richard Harding Davis and Jack London. He also extracted some extraordinary stories out of his experiences in Vera Cruz, and he wrote a play about Davis, and published, in all, more than a dozen stories based upon his experiences in Mexico. The one story he neglected to explore fully was that of the battle of Xochimilco, in which he was wounded. In retrospect, he was rather saddened to recollect that two men were actually killed in this mock battle, and he admitted to being rather foolhar'y, but the ludicrous aspects of the affair were omitted in the sensationalized dispatches that he and two fellow reporters sent back from the front.

Starrett was assigned to a beat in Washington after his return from Mexico, and he liked to recollect his friendly encounters with the then Assistant Secretary of the Navy, Franklin Delano Roosevelt. His encounters with President Wilson were somewhat less friendly, although he greatly admired the President, and his meetings with William Jennings Bryan were altogether unsatisfactory.

But the highlight of his Washington experience was the discovery that one of the writers he greatly admired, Ambrose Bierce, had disappeared in Mexico. Starrett was the reporter who broke this story to the world; it appeared on the front page of the *Daily News*. Bierce's fate is still unknown, and a great deal of copy has been written on the mystery since Starrett's initial public announcement. Starrett later published a superb long essay on Bierce, and he was Bierce's first and foremost bibliographer. Bierce's popularity today is largely accountable to the fact that Starrett's keen sensibility defined the best of Bierce, and marked him as one of the more important authors of his time. Starrett did virtually the same for Stephen Crane and others, and his contribution in this area of discovery has never been properly recognized.

Starrett returned from his second Mexican campaign and began to write again for the magazines. He sold enough stories to consider retiring from journalism and devoting all of his time to literature, or forms of literature. He wanted to be a good writer, or even a great one, and had time and circumstance treated him more kindly, he would have been one of the finest novelists of the century. He proved that he could write an intriguing quality novel when, in 1928, he published *Seaports in the Moon*, a book that Herbert Gorman called, "A supreme and credible flight of fantasy, brilliantly structured in a style of classic mold and articulation."

The book was Starrett's dominant bid for literary recognition, and it was well received by the critics. But the sales were insufficient to permit the author to continue with a second literary novel, and he turned again to the stories and articles that paid his way and permitted him to involve himself in literary scholarship.

Starrett was a significant force in the literary life of Chicago. He was present when noteworthy events took place, when *Poetry* and the *Little Review* were founded, when O'Brien's *Art* and Kirch's *The Lantern* came into being, when his own magazine, *The Wave*, rippled in the fermenting sea of the city's cultural expansion. Starrett, of course, knew all of the important writers in Chicago; moreover, he knew many celebrated European authors, several of whom were destined to have a strong influence on his life and work.

Among the latter was Sir Arthur Conan Doyle, who favored Starrett's stimulating pioneering research on his most popular creation, Sherlock Holmes. Starrett had read the stories of the world's greatest private detective when he was a boy of scarcely ten, and it was the beginning of what he referred to as "a lifetime of Conan Doyle idolatry." His own great work on the subject was *The Private Life of Sherlock Holmes*, the first biography of a fictional character ever written. This was the outgrowth of a series of superb essays that he began publishing as early as 1918, and the book itself appeared in 1933. It was an immediate success.

It was with the publication of *The Private Life*, and his masterful pastiche *The Unique Hamlet*, along with his widely anthologized poem 221-B, and his numerous scholarly essays on Holmes, that Starrett came to be dignified further as the "Dean" of Sherlockians, the foremost scholar on Sherlock Holmes in the world.

People from many foreign countries wrote to him with questions about Sherlock Holmes; the surprising thing was that any one man could answer all of the questions asked. Starrett also seemed to take on the character and personality of Holmes, and if any off-stage personage merited this identification through manner, appearance, and brilliance of mind, it was Starrett. Some devotées of the detective even insisted that Starrett *was* Holmes. There may have been times when he himself believed it, for his habits, and his penchant for discovery, and the high cultural posture of his mind—the confluence of these, and his reading on the subject—conditioned his manner of speech, outlook, even dress, so that he was almost a twentieth century anachronism. Caricatures of him as Holmes were drawn by famous artists and cartoonists, and the ever-growing membership of the Baker Street Irregulars, the Sherlockian society that he helped found, regarded him, and quite properly, with particular reverence and acclaim.

It can be said without qualification that those who knew Starrett's wide-ranging scholarship on Holmes must inevitably canonize, or Conanize, him; after all, it derived from their soaring respect for the man. For them, Starrett could do no wrong; and the incredible thing was, they were probably right. Starrett's gentility, his benign and sympathetic perspective, his kindliness and aristocratic grace—all that characterized him so individualistically—remained with him throughout life.

Starrett's Conan Doyle idolatry, after all, derived from his affinity for a man whose standards were not unlike his own. Doyle's first friendly letter to Starrett was written soon after Starrett's review of *His Last Bow* in 1917. Doyle, at that time, was finished with Sherlock Holmes, and Starrett was just beginning. He met Doyle once, briefly, but was denied the opportunity to talk with him at length about Sherlock. Doyle, by then, did not discuss his great detective.

The Baker Street Irregulars, a society of which Starrett was one of the early decisive members, began in 1933, with Christopher Morley's Bowling Green department in the *Saturday Review of Literature*. The society was dedicated to a study of the Sacred Writings, the sixty stories about Holmes. The members exchanged scholarly observations and wrote "papers" for their mutual edification. Their first formal meeting was held at Cella's restaurant in New York on June 5, 1934; their first state dinner took place there in December of that year and it was, indeed, an historic occasion.

Starrett had invited the great actor William Gillette to be his guest, along with Alexander Woollcott. To the latter, Starrett suggested that a hansom cab might be appropriate for their journey down Fifth Avenue. Starrett arrived at Wollcott's East 52nd Street apartment and was dragged into a bedroom where he was fitted with a deerstalker cap and cape; Woollcott, similarly attired, rushed him down to the street. There were two hansom cabs waiting. The first drove off without an occupant. "Always take the second cab," Woollcott said, quoting Holmes. "The first may be dangerous." He told the second driver to follow the first.

They arrived at Cella's for what was to become a legendary dinner. Morley was there, of course, and Henry Morton Robinson, Elmer Davis, Frederic Dorr Steele the artist, Dr. Gray Chandler Briggs of St. Louis, Harold Bell, and eight others. Gillette was absent. At least for the moment. They all became slightly oiled, and Starrett is said to have crawled about on the floor on all fours in imitation of the Hound of the Baskervilles—an allegation he stoutly denied—prior to falling asleep, an allegation he admitted to; and then Gillette arrived. The door flew open and there he stood, not Gillette any longer, but Sherlock Holmes!

After that, the Baker Street Irregulars flourished, accumulating offshoot societies throughout the world. Boston and Chicago were the first to follow the BSI, Starrett founding the latter, the Hounds (sic) of the Baskerville, and Starrett once remarked that if the membership continued to accelerate, they would soon have enough to swing a presidential election. It is a rather elite and spirited membership, one that attracts exceptional participants, who must, of course, subscribe to the underlying theme that glorifies Holmes as a private detective non pareil.

In 1935 Starrett, who had earned some money with one of his mystery novels, added to that accrued from the sale of hundreds of stories, took off for what was reputedly a three-month round-the-world cruise. He found China enough of a magnet to hold him for more than two years. In a stopover in Toyko, he was refused admittance to a hotel because he registered as Vincent Starrett. The matter was finally cleared up when an American consular official who knew Starrett's work vouched for him; they learned that there was another man, of differing physiognomy, whose name also happened to be Vincent Starrett.

The Japanese exposed Starrett to some petty espionage until a news article appeared heralding him as a great American detective story writer and a former policeman, whose words about the Japanese police system were very complimentary. He was treated quite well after that, but his real objective was a visit with Lin Yutang in China. He and the popular Chinese writer became fast friends. He did considerable research on the Chinese detective story, and was the first writer in English to provide any definite statement on that obscure subject. Starrett was becoming one of the foremost authorities on the detective story per se, an erudition that led to countless writing assignments for him in years to come. Three books came out of his experiences in China, the most notable being *Murder in Peking*, a novel that caused considerable excitement when it was alleged to be based on an actual murder that had taken place.

Leaving China, Starrett spent six weeks in Italy, seeing Mussolini, who did not impress him, and the graves of Keats, Shelly, and one of his favorite authors, Robert Ballantyne. But it was London where he was to make one of his extraordinary discoveries. Following through on a reference in Washington Irving to Dame Quickly's "parcel-gilt goblet" and a curious tobacco box on which the Boar's Head Tavern was depicted, he tracked them both down to a church in Eastcheap; later he wrote one of his superb essays of discovery about them.

Before departing from England, he met with some of his most admired correspondents and made a Dickens pilgrimage. Characteristic of all of his adventures, each bore fruit in a later essay, story, or book.

In his absence from America, the detective story genre had changed, but he continued to write and sell his own stories while working on what he regarded as the more serious literary essay. This post-China period was a prolific and remunerative time for Starrett, for he published more than half a dozen books in as many years, including books of poetry, literary essays, detective stories, and one juvenile. He had begun writing a series of short essays on the outstanding books of the century, and these, when collected in a Bantam paperback, became one of his best-selling volumes. He was being called the "Number One American Bookman," and he doubtlessly deserved the title because of his vast knowledge of and affection for books. Two other exceptional books of essays grew out of his book columns that appeared regularly for a number of years and won immense popularity. And at this time, in the early '40s, he was commissioned to write introductions to many quality editions of works by Dickens, Wilkie Collins, Poe, John McCutcheon, and, it need hardly be said, Conan Doyle.

Starrett began to gain recognition for his columns and his later work, particularly his books about books and his Sherlockian reveries. Starrett was to gain identity as the dean of Chicago authors, a designation to which he did not object, but the fact was, he did not like to think that this was the culmination of his career. Indeed, Starrett continued to write and write well until his eighty-sixth year. At the age of eighty-four he began a remarkable series of essays.

At the time of his death he had more than eight books in print. There are more to come. He left several unpublished works that, it is hoped, will soon appear in printed form. It may require a decade or half a century, but Starrett will be recognized in time as one of this century's great bibliographical scholars and literary essayists; he shall also gain further credit for his formative efforts in Holmesian scholarship, not to mention the vast erudition and individuality of style that can be found in his works on Poe, Stevenson, Machen, Bierce, Crane, and others.

The figure of Vincent Starrett will gain dominance against the somewhat shadowy background of Chicago's literary life in the first half of the twentieth century. There are many who knew and revered him. He died on the fortieth anniversary of the annual Baker Street Irregular banquet in New York; it is certain that at all subsequent dinners his name will be advanced with that of his favorite, Sherlock Holmes.

In his final years, I had the rare privilege of being with him almost daily. I recall incidents that were both amusing and touchingly tragic. I can remember one morning when he got up reciting verse after verse of Shelley; I recall his vivid recollections of his past, and his joy in touring again those environs of his youth in Oak Park and Austin; I was with him when his beloved wife Ray (for Rachel) died, and his comments at the time on life and death were brilliant and disquieting. I restrained him from taking his own life one insane gray afternoon; I knew the joy he took in life, in books, in people, in small animals and children. He was a unique and gifted man who upheld the dignity and the standards of fairness and honor that seem now to have belonged to an earlier century. He had gentility and a true aristocratic carriage and perspective. He was somebody above the common lot, but he would never proclaim it. It wasn't long after my first meeting with him, now more than twenty-five years ago, that he proceeded to assist me. I was a beginning writer then, and Vincent Starrett gave me an objective and directions on how to get there. I didn't know then that he was a genius; I thought I was the genius. But Vincent was always the maestro and I the ungrateful student. There was one thing he taught me that I did not reject and that was himself; I was privileged to receive that from him. That was the best you could have from Vincent Starrett: himself. What a fine man, what a great writer, what a unique and incredibly gentle person he was. Of Sherlock Holmes, Starrett wrote, "Ave, Sherlock. We who will someday pass and be forgotten salute you, undying."

Ave, Vincent . . . Like that house in Baker Street where Vincent's favorite fictional character lived, Vincent Starrett, the biographer of Sherlock Holmes, will continue to be remembered as long as books are written and read.

EPILOGUE

Vincent Starrett entertained certain emendations in *The Private Life of Sherlock Holmes*. He was addicted to refinement, in both his life and his writing, and he had never persuaded himself that there were not improvements he could bring to this rendering. He question-marked particular issues in the hope of resolving them at a future date: they are far too complex to justify extended comment here, but a few points may be made with respect to what they reveal of Starrett's postures as both a literary genius and a man of exceptional gentility.

In his sentimental way, for example, he wanted to add the name of his friend Basil Rathbone to the "In Memoriam." He would have added others as well. "The Unique Hamlet," that incomparable pastiche, is a classic, but Vincent Starrett had it in his plans to rewrite it, making certain changes of a scholarly nature as well as syntactical refinements. It must be remembered that this was a very early work: indeed, perhaps the very first of its kind. Starrett's style in later years was more sophisticated, and his perspective on his early writings quite critical: he was constantly disposed toward revisions, trying for perfection.

In connection with "pastiche" itself, it is appropriate to quote from a letter Starrett received from his friend and fellow tradesman, H. Bedford-Jones. Starrett and Bedford-Jones exchanged a good many pleasantries over the years and participated in more than a few ingenious hoaxes:

My dear Starrett:
As a novitiate irregular of your Baskervilles I should like to make myself unpopular by registering a protest against the use of the word "pastiche" by you and other Baker Street Irregulars. It is extensively used in referring to any monograph anent Mr. Holmes and his doings. The members mouth it with great unction, as a dog falls upon some ancient bone he has disinterred; yet, I think, such use of this French-Italian slang word is improper. It has a derogatory sense, one of caricature. It is a fossilized dinosaur bone.
. . . does not Holmes mention his own monograph touching upon this very word and its improper usages?
. . . the views of Dr. Conan Doyle himself might be adduced in this respect! I refrain from quoting them here, as occurring in a private communication, and to save space. However, the protest is registered.
H. Bedford-Jones

Returning to the question of emendations contemplated by Vincent Starrett in his work, he made notations that would fall into the arena of the "higher criticism," but these are better reserved for a forum like *The Baker Street Journal,* that thesaurus for all erudite and discerning students of Conanical verities. Starrett was aware of the questions, of course, and constantly in search of the answers; that he had little time to incorporate the answers in a further revised text is accountable to the fact that he received literally thousands of letters that proffered countless other questions, most of which he made a great effort to answer. He had no secretary to do that work for him; there were times when he had little money for the postage to carry his response back to the inquiring party. He would have given us a great deal more on the literary side if he had been less of a gentleman; but then any less a gentleman would not have been Vincent Starrett.

Whatever changes he might have made in this masterful work, they would not have discredited the brilliance of his initial achievement. Vincent Starrett was the only man who could have written *The Private Life of Sherlock Holmes*.

—MICHAEL MURPHY

VINCENT STARRETT'S PERSONAL BOOKPLATE,
AS EXECUTED BY THE WELL-KNOWN
ILLUSTRATOR AND AUTHOR,
FRIDOLF JOHNSON

Selective Reading

List of Writings on

Conan Doyle,

Sherlock Holmes,

and Dr. Watson

The reader of this classic book on Sherlock Holmes may find his appetite sufficiently aroused to seek out other illuminating works on the subject. The list is less for the scholar than for the searching reader, disposed to adventure as well as diversion, the reader who values the enduring experience that only the printed word can provide.

Some of the works in this list are out of print and difficult to find; the best sources for those are used book dealers and B.S.I. scion society publications.

I am grateful to Bob Hahn, Sir Hugo of Hugo's Companions, Chicago, whose judgment was invaluable in the preparation of this list.

—Michael Murphy

The Baker Street Four Wheeler. Edited by Edgar Smith, Pamphlet House, 1944. (Cornerstone work.)

Baker Street Studies. Edited by H. W. Bell. Constable and Co., 1934. (Cornerstone.)

Baring-Gould, William. *The Annotated Sherlock Holmes.* Clarkson Potter, 1967.

———. *The Chronological Sherlock Holmes.* (Privately printed, 1955.)

———. *The Sherlock Holmes of Baker Street.* Clarkson Potter, 1942. Popular Library, 1963.

Biography

Doyle, Arthur Conan. *Memories and Adventures.* Hodder and Stoughton, 1924; Little Brown, 1924. Doyle's autobiography.

Doyle, Adrian Conan. *The True Conan Doyle.* John Murray, 1945. (Reverential, to say the least.)

Carr, John Dickson. *The Life of Sir Arthur Conan Doyle.* Harper and Brothers, 1934. (The best of the biographies to date.)

Nordon, Pierre. *Conan Doyle.* Holt, Rinehart and Winston, 1947. (A superb biography.)

Pearson, Hesketh. *Conan Doyle—Life and Art.* Methuen and Co., 1943. Guild Books, London, 1946. (An entertaining but relatively superficial biography.)

Blakeney, T. S. *Sherlock Holmes: Fact and Fiction*. John Murray, 1932. (Cornerstone collection of critical essays.)

Boucher, Anthony. *The Case of the Baker Street Irregulars*. Simon and Schuster, 1940. Collier Books (paperback), 1962.

Brend, Gavin *My Dear Holmes*. George Allen and Unwin, 1951. (Cornerstone work.)

Carr, John Dickson (with Adrian Conan Doyle). *The Exploits of Sherlock Holmes*. Random House, 1954. (New adventures with Holmes, in the manner of, but not on the level of, the master's work.)

Clarke, R. W. *Best of the Pips*. (Privately printed, 1955.) (A collection of commentaries by one of the early and most exclusive scion societies, the Westchester County Pips.)

Christ, Jay Finley. *An Irregular Chronology of Sherlock Holmes*. Fanlight House, 1947. (Cornerstone work that provides a chronology of the stories by one of the great early scholars in the field.)

————. *An Irregular Guide to Sherlock Holmes of Baker Street*. Argus Books, 1947. (Cornerstone.)

Dakin, Martin. *A Sherlock Holmes Commentary*. Drake, 1972. (An engaging work.)

Derleth, August. The *Solar Pons* stories, representing varied and delightful pastiches, are directly inspired by The Sherlock Holmes saga, and are being issued by Pinnacle Books in series.

Farmer, Philip José. *The Peerless Peers*. Aspen Press, 1974. (A superior pastiche.)

Fish, Robert L. *The Incredible Schlock Homes*. Simon and Schuster, 1966.

————. *The Memoirs of Schlock Homes*. Simon and Schuster, 1974. (Among the most ingenious and amusing pastiches.)

Gardner, John. *The Return of Moriarty*. Putnam's Sons, 1974.

Hall, R. Trevor. *Sherlock Holmes: Ten Literary Studies*. Bodley Head, 1970.

————. *The Late Sherlock Holmes*. Duckworth Books, 1971.

Hardwicke, Michael and Molly. *The Man Who Was Sherlock Holmes*. Doubleday and Co., 1964.

————. *The Sherlock Holmes Companion*. Doubleday and Co., 1963.

Harrison, Michael. *In the Footsteps of Sherlock Holmes*. Caszell and Co., 1960 (highly recommended). Revised edition, Drake, 1972.

————. *London by Gaslight*. Davies, 1963.

Holroyd, James. *Baker Street Byways*. Allen and Unwin, 1959. (Cornerstone work.)

The Incunabular Holmes. Edited by Edgar Smith. B.S.I., 1958. (Cornerstone.)

Introducing Mr. Sherlock Holmes. Edited by Edgar Smith. B.S.I., 1959. (Cornerstone.)

Jaffee, Irving. *Elementary, My Dear Watson.* Theodore Gans and Sons, 1965. (Relatively minor collection of essays.)

Jaffee, Irving and Mary. *Beyond Baker Street.* Pontine Press, 1973.

Klinefelter, Walter. *Sherlock Holmes in Portrait and Profile.* Syracuse University Press, 1963. Introduction by Vincent Starrett. (The major work on the illustrators of Holmes.)

Knox, Msgr. Ronald. *Essays in Satire.* Sheed and Ward, 1928. (A collection of the early parodies and light-hearted renderings. Cornerstone).

Lauritzen, Henry. *Mr. Sherlock Holmes.* (Privately printed, 1968.)

――――. *My Dear Watson* (Privately printed in Danish.) (Representative of the best of the foreign work on Holmes, of which there is a vast quantity in virtually every language.)

Lauterback, Charles. *The Baker Street Ballads.* Pontine Press, 1971. (A collection of original verse.)

Lewis, Arthur. *The Copper Beeches.* Trident Press, 1971. (A well-written novel in which the Baker Street Irregulars are central to the story evolvement.)

McQueen, Ian. *Sherlock Holmes Detected.* Drake, 1974.

Meyer, Nicholas. *The Seven Per-cent Solution.* Dutton, 1974. (The current bestseller.)

The Misadventures of Sherlock Holmes. Edited by Ellery Queen. Little Brown, 1944. (One of the first collections of pastiches, now rare because of suppression on questions of copyright.)

Parks, Orlando. *Mr. Sherlock Holmes and Dr. John H. Watson, An Encyclopedia of Their Affairs.* Northwestern University Press. (An extensive and eminently readable index.)

Roberts, S. C. *Dr. Watson: Prolegomena to the Study of a Biographical Problem.* Faber and Faber, 1931. (Cornerstone work.)

Sayers, Dorothy. *Unpopular Opinions.* Golancz, 1946. (A cornerstone assembly of scholarly essays.)

Science Fictional Sherlock Holmes. Edited by Ann Metcalfe. (Privately printed, 1960.)

Second Cab. Edited by James Keddie. (Privately printed, 1947). (Cornerstone.)

Sherlockian Studies. Edited by Robert Cutter. (Privately printed, 1947.)

Smith, Edgar. *Holmes and Watson, A Miscellany.* Oxford University Press, 1953.

———. *A Baker Street Folio: Edited Letters of Franklin D. Roosevelt on the B.S.I.* Published by the B.S.I., 1945.

————. *Baker Street and Beyond—A Sherlockian Gazateer*. Pamphlet House, 1940.

————. *A Baker Street Inventory*. Pamphlet House, 1945.

(Anything written or edited by Smith is worth reading and keeping; one of the most devoted Sherlockians.)

Starrett, Vincent. *Bookman's Holiday*. Random House, 1942. (Includes classic commentary on Sherlock Holmes, among other fascinating recollections of adventures in reading.)

————(editor). *221–B, Studies in Sherlock Holmes*. Macmillan, 1940. (Handsome reprint, Biblo and Tannen, 1970.)

————. *Books and Bipeds*. Argus, 1947. (A selection of columns that includes, inevitably, several on Holmes.)

————. *Late, Later and Possibly Last*. Essays by Vincent Starret. Autolycus, 1973. Limited, 500 signed. (Contains Starrett's last essay on Holmes, a masterpiece.)

————. *Encomiums for Vincent Starret*. The Printery, Kirkwood, Mo., 1975. Limited, 210 copies. (Probably the most beautiful book on Starrett ever published, hand-set and bound by hand. Fine Sherlockian content.)

————. *The Unique Hamlet*. Walter Hill, 1920. Limited, 200 copies. (The first quality pastiche, a classic, reprinted in this volume.)

Van Liere, Dr. Edward J. *A Doctor Enjoys Sherlock Holmes*. Vantage Press, 1960.

Wallace, Irving. *The Fabulous Originals.* (As well as the present work, has important biographical references to Doyle.)

Warrick, Guy. *Sherlock Holmes and Music.* Faber and Faber, 1957. (A specialized study.)

Waal, Ronald de. *A World Bibliography of Sherlock Holmes and Dr. Watson.* New York Graphic Society, 1974. (The definitive bibliography, a work long in progress and high in price.)

Periodicals

Periodicals (a number of periodicals continue to be devoted to the subject, this list representing several of the more important.)

Baker Street Journal. Old Series, New York, 1946–1948. Edited by Edgar Smith.

Baker Street Journal. New Series, New York, 1949—. (Published quarterly.) Edited by Edgar Smith and, in later years, by Dr. Julian Wolff. *The* publication for the growing Sherlockian.

Sherlock Holmes Journal. London. Edited by Lord Donegall. (British counterpart to BSJ.)

Devon County Chronical. Chicago. R. Hahn, editor.

Vermissa Herald. San Francisco. W. Berner, editor.

West by One and by One. An Anthology of Irregular Writings, 1965—. Representing the Scowrers and

Molly Mcguires of San Francisco and the Trained Cormorants of Los Angeles.

The Holmes Canon

Anyone reading a selection of works in the preceding list should necessarily read the Sherlock Holmes stories. The accepted definitive edition is that first issued by Doubleday in 1936, two volumes, with a magnificent introduction by Christopher Morley.

There are a number of other single and multi-volume editions. Among the best is the three-volume Heritage Press edition of 1950, with the introduction by Vincent Starrett, an edition not easily come upon. But for the reader who has not read the stories, any edition, any condition, will be more than adequate—likely he will seek out improved editions as he becomes more and more magnetized by the world's most popular and enduring private consulting detective.

The fascinating story behind
the greatest naval adventures of all time.
the saga of Horatio Hornblower

P440 $1.95

The
Hornblower
Companion

C. S. FORESTER

The complete and indispensable guide.
Fully illustrated with maps, charts, and drawings
by Samuel H. Bryant

P440   THE HORNBLOWER COMPANION $1.95

TO ORDER

Please check the space next to the book/s you want, send this order
form together with your check or money order, include the price of
the book/s and 25¢ for handling and mailing to:

PINNACLE BOOKS, INC. / P.O. Box 4347
Grand Central Station / New York, N.Y. 10017

☐ CHECK HERE IF YOU WANT A FREE CATALOG

I have enclosed $＿＿＿＿＿check＿＿＿＿＿or money order＿＿＿＿＿
as payment in full. No C.O.D.'s

Name＿＿＿＿＿＿＿＿＿＿＿＿＿＿＿＿＿＿＿＿＿＿＿＿＿＿＿＿

Address＿＿＿＿＿＿＿＿＿＿＿＿＿＿＿＿＿＿＿＿＿＿＿＿＿＿

City＿＿＿＿＿＿＿＿＿＿State＿＿＿＿＿＿Zip＿＿＿＿＿＿＿
(Please allow time for delivery)